Repent & Believe

by Derek Prince

"Repent ye, and believe the gospel."
Mark 1:15

ISBN NO. 0-934920-01-X

TABLE OF CONTENTS

PREFACE — Page 5

I—REPENTANCE — Page 7
Explained From Greek and Hebrew - Distinguished From Remorse - The Sinner's First Response To God - The Only Way To True Faith

II—FAITH — Page 18
Bible Definition - Distinguished From Hope - Based Solely On God's Word - Expressed By Confession

III—FAITH — Page 29
Its Unique And Supreme Importance - The Only Basis Of All Righteous Living - Appropriating All God's Promises

IV—FAITH FOR SALVATION — Page 40
The Four Basic Facts Of The Gospel - The Simple Act Of Appropriation

V—FAITH AND WORKS — Page 51
Salvation By Faith Alone - Living Faith Always Expressed And Developed By Works

VI—LAW AND GRACE — Page 62
The Law Of Moses One Single Complete System - Given Only To Israel - Does Not Apply To Christians

VII—THE PURPOSE OF THE LAW — Page 72
To Reveal Sin - To Prove Man's Inability To Save Himself - To Foreshow Christ - To Preserve Israel - Perfectly Fulfilled By Christ

VIII—THE TRUE RIGHTEOUSNESS — Page 82
The Two Great Commandments - Love The Fulfilling Of The Law - The New Testament Pattern Of Obedience

DEREK PRINCE
King's Scholar, Eton College
B.A., M.A. Cambridge
Formerly
Fellow of King's College,
Cambridge

ABOUT THE AUTHOR

Derek Prince was born in India, of British parents. He was educated as a scholar of Greek and Latin at two of Britain's most famous educational institutions - Eton College and Cambridge University. From 1940 to 1949, he held a Fellowship (equivalent to a resident professorship) in Ancient and Modern Philosophy at King's College, Cambridge. He also studied Hebrew and Aramaic, both at Cambridge University and at the Hebrew University in Jerusalem. In addition, he speaks a number of other modern languages.

In the early years of World War II, while serving as a hospital attendant with the British Army, Derek Prince experienced a life-changing encounter with Jesus Christ, concerning which, he writes:

Out of this encounter, I formed two conclusions which I have never since had reason to change: first, that Jesus Christ is alive; second, that the Bible is a true, relevant, up-to-date book. These two conclusions radically and permanently altered the whole course of my life.

At the end of World War II, he remained where the British Army had placed him - in Jerusalem. Through his marriage to his first wife, Lydia, he became father to the eight adopted girls in Lydia's children's home there. Together, the family saw the rebirth of the State of Israel in 1948.

While serving as educator in Kenya, Derek and Lydia adopted their ninth child, an African baby girl. Lydia died in 1975, and Derek Prince married his present wife, Ruth, in 1978.

In the intervening years, Derek Prince has served as pastor, educator, lecturer, and counselor on several continents, and is internationally recognized as one of the leading Bible expositors of our time. He has authored over 20 books, many of which have been translated into other languages. In great demand as a conference speaker, Derek Prince travels frequently to many other parts of the world, and also maintains a base in Israel.

Non-denominational and non-sectarian in his approach, Derek Prince has prophetic insight into the significance of current events in the light of Bible prophecy.

* * * * *

With a few changes, these messages are printed here exactly as they were delivered over the air on the Study Hour radio program.

I
Repentance

Explained From Greek And Hebrew—Distinguished From Remorse—The Sinner's First Response To God—The Only Way To True Faith

Welcome to the Study Hour.

Our textbook—the Bible.

We are continuing today with our series entitled "Foundations." Our study today will be the ninth in this particular series.*

In this series we commenced by examining the basic foundation of the Christian faith, and we saw that this foundation is none other than Christ Himself—Christ revealed, and Christ received into the heart and life of each individual believer.

Thereafter we saw that the process of building upon this foundation of Christ in our lives consists of actively studying and applying the teaching of the Bible. Thus, as the apostle Paul tells us in Acts chapter 20, verse 32, it is God's Word, the Bible, which is able to **build us up** and to give us our inheritance in Christ.

In the last five studies in this series we have examined a number of definite, practical effects which God's Word produces in us, as, with faith and obedience, we receive and apply its teaching. In these five studies we have enumerated altogether nine different ways in which the Bible works in the believer, nine different beneficial results which it produces. These nine results of the Bible's working in us are as follows:

First, faith; second, the new birth; third, complete spiritual nourishment; fourth, healing and health for our physical bodies; fifth, mental illumination and understanding; sixth, victory over sin and Satan; seventh, cleansing

*The first eight studies in this series are published as a book, under the title: "FOUNDATION FOR FAITH." See back cover of this book.

page seven

and sanctification; eighth, a mirror of inward spiritual revelation; ninth, our judge.

Now at this stage in our studies, someone might quite reasonably say: "You have told us that Christ is the foundation of the Christian faith; you have told us that we build upon this foundation in our lives by studying and applying the teachings of the Bible; you have told us various different results which the Bible will produce in us as we study and apply it in this way. I agree with all this, but I need to know more definitely which of the Bible's doctrines I should begin to study first. All that you have told us so far about studying has been quite general. When we wish to begin studying the Bible in detail, is there some way of knowing which are the basic doctrines, that are more important than others, and which should therefore be studied first, before any of the others?"

This is a reasonable and practical question, and like all such questions related to the study of the Bible, an answer to it may be found within the pages of the Bible itself. The Bible does clearly state that certain of its doctrines are more basic and important than the rest, and should therefore be studied first. In fact, the Bible actually gives a definite list of six such basic, or foundation, doctrines. The passage where this list is found is Hebrews chapter 6, verses 1 and 2, where we read:

"Therefore leaving the principles of the doctrine of Christ, let us go on unto perfection; not laying again the foundation of repentance from dead works, and of faith toward God, of the doctrine of baptisms, and of laying on of hands, and of resurrection of the dead, and of eternal judgment."

In the margin of the standard King James Version, the alternative reading suggested for "the principles of the doctrine of Christ" is "the word of the beginning of Christ." This brings out the point that we are here dealing with the doctrines which should constitute the beginning—the starting off point—in our study of Christ and His teaching as a whole. This point is further emphasized by the use, in the same verse, of the phrase, "the foundation." The writer of Hebrews is setting two thoughts side by side: first, the laying of the right doctrinal foundation; second, going on after this to perfection; that is, to a completed edifice of Christian doctrine and conduct. The purpose of his exhortation is that we should "go on unto perfection"; that is, to the completed edifice. But he makes it plain that we cannot hope to do this, unless we have first laid a complete and stable foundation of the basic doctrines.

In speaking of this foundation of basic doctrines, the writer lists in order the following six successive doctrines: First, "repentance from dead works"; second, "faith toward God"; third, "the doctrine of baptisms"; fourth, "laying on of hands"; fifth, "ressurection of the dead"; sixth, "eternal judgment." More briefly, we might summarize these basic doctrines as follows: First, repentance; second, faith; third, baptism; fourth, laying on of hands; fifth, resurrection; sixth, judgment.

We have now reached the place in our studies where it is appropriate for us to examine each of these six doctrines in order; and today we shall commence with the first of these doctrines, "Repentance," or, more fully, "Repentance from dead works."

* * *

First of all, it is important to arrive at a clear understanding of the true meaning of the word "Repentance," as used in the scripture.

In the New Testament, the English verb "to repent" is normally used to translate the Greek verb "metanoein." Now this Greek verb "metanoein" has one clear, definite meaning all through the history of the Greek language, right through Classical Greek and down into New Testament Greek. Its basic meaning is always the same: "to change one's mind." Thus, the basic significance of "repentance" in the New Testament is not an emotion, but a **decision**. It is most important to be clear about this fact, because it serves to dispel many false impressions and ideas connected with "repentance." Many people associate "repentance" primarily with emotion—with the shedding of tears—and so on. But it is possible for a person to feel great emotion and to shed many tears, and yet never to repent, in the true scriptural sense. Other people, again, associate repentance with the carrying out of special religious rites or ordinances—with what is called "doing penance." But here, too, the same applies: it is possible to go through many religious rites and ordinances, and yet never to repent, in the true scriptural sense. True repentance is just this one thing: a firm inward decision—a change of mind.

If we turn back to the Old Testament, we find that the word there most commonly translated "to repent" means literally "to turn," "to return," "to turn back." This harmonizes perfectly with the meaning of repentance as revealed in the New Testament. The New Testament word denotes the inner decision, the inner change of mind; the Old Testament word denotes the outward action which is the expression of the inward change of mind—the act of turning back, of turning around. Thus, the New Testament emphasizes the inward nature of true repentance; the Old Testament emphasizes the outward expression in action of the inner change. Putting the two together, we form this complete picture of repentance: repentance is an inner change of mind, resulting in an outward turning back, or turning around, to face and to move in a completely new direction.

The perfect example of true repentance, defined in this way, is found in the parable of the prodigal son, as related by Jesus in Luke chapter 15, verses 11 through 32. Here we read how the prodigal turned his back on father and home, and went far off into a distant land, there to waste all that he had in sin and dissipation. Eventually he came to himself, hungry, lonely, and in rags, sitting among the swine, longing for something to fill his belly. At this point we read, in verse 18, that he made a decision. He said, "I will arise and go to my father . . . " Furthermore, we read in verse 20 that he immediately carried out his decision: "And he arose, and came to his father." This is true repentance: first, the inward decision; then, the outward act of carrying out that decision—the act of turning back to father and home.

In his own natural, unregenerate, sinful condition, every man that was ever born has turned his back on God, his Father, and on heaven, his home. In this condition, each step that he takes is a step away from God and from heaven. As he walks this way, the light is behind him and the shadows are before him. The further he goes, the longer and darker the shadows become. Each step that he takes is one step nearer the end—one step nearer the grave, nearer hell, nearer the endless darkness of a lost eternity. For every man that takes this course, there is one thing that he must do first, one essential act that he must make. He must stop, he must change his mind, change his direction, turn back, turn around, face the opposite way, turn his back to the shadows and face toward the light. This first, essential act is called in the scripture "repentance." It is the first move that any sinner must make who desires to be reconciled with God.

Of course, there are some passages in the scripture where we find the verb "to repent" used in a different sense, but when we examine these passages carefully, we find that the English word "to repent" is used to translate some other word in the original language. For example, we read in Matthew chapter 27, verses 3 and 4, that Judas Iscariot, when he saw that Christ had been condemned to death, afterwards repented of his part in betraying Christ for money. "Then Judas, which had betrayed him, when he saw that he was condemned, repented himself, and brought again the thirty pieces of silver to the chief priests and elders, saying, I have sinned in that I have betrayed the innocent blood. And they said, What is that to us? See thou to that."

Here we read that "Judas repented himself." But the Greek word used in the original is not the word "metanoein," of which we have already said that it means a decision, a change of mind. The Greek word here used of Judas, "metamelein," denotes that which people often wrongly interpret as repentance, that is, emotion, remorse, anguish. There is no doubt that at this moment Judas experienced intense anguish and remorse. Nevertheless, he did not experience true, scriptural repentance; he did not change his mind, his course, his direction. On the contrary, we read in the very next verse, that he went and hanged himself; and in Acts chapter 1, verse 25, this is expressed by the words, "Judas by transgression fell, that he might go to his own place." Certainly, Judas experienced emotion—strong emotion—bitter anguish and remorse. But he did not experience true repentance; he did not change his mind, his course. The truth is that he could not change his course; he had already gone too far; in spite of the Saviour's warning, he had deliberately committed himself to a course from which there could afterwards be no return. He had passed "the place of repentance." What a terrible and solemn lesson there is in this! It is possible for a man, by stubborn and wilful continuance in his own way, to come to a place from which there is no turning back—a place where the door of repentance has, by his own wilfulness, been forever slammed shut behind him.

In Hebrews chapter 12, verses 16 and 17, we read of another man who made this same tragic error. That man was "Esau, who for one morsel of meat sold his birthright." The writer of Hebrews then continues: "For ye know how that afterwards, when he would have inherited the blessing, he was rejected: for he found no place of repentance, though he sought it carefully with tears." In a foolish, careless moment Esau had parted with his birthright, as the firstborn son of Isaac, to his brother Jacob, in exchange for a mere bowl of soup. In relating this incident, the scripture records in Genesis chapter 25, verse 34: "Thus Esau despised his birthright"—and we must remember that in despising his birthright, he despised all the blessings and the promises of God that were associated with the birthright. Later, Esau regretted what he had done. He sought to regain the birthright and the blessing; he sought it carefully with tears; yet he was rejected. Why? Because he found no place of repentance (in the margin of the King James Version the alternative translation is: "He found no way to change his mind."). Here is further evidence that strong emotion is not necessarily proof of repentance. Esau cried aloud and shed bitter tears. But in spite of all this, he found no place of re- of repentance, of changing his mind. By a seemingly trivial and unimportant act he had decided the whole course of his life, and his destiny both for time and for eternity. He had committed himself to a course from which afterwards he could find no way of return.

How many men today do just the same as Esau! For a few moments of sensual pleasure or carnal indulgence, for something so cheap as a cigarette, or a glass of beer or whiskey—they despise all the blessings and promises of almighty God. Later, when they feel their mistake, when they begin to long after and to cry out for those spiritual and eternal blessings which they had despised, to their dismay they find themselves rejected. Why? Because they can find no place of repentance, no way to change their minds.

* * *

The whole record of the New Testament is absolutely unanimous on this one point: True repentance must always go before true faith; without true repentance there can never be true faith.

The call to repentance begins at the very introduction to the New Testament, with the ministry of John the Baptist. In Mark's Gospel chapter 1, verses 3 and 4, we read: "The voice of one crying in the wilderness, Prepare ye the way of the Lord, make his paths straight. John did baptize in the wilderness, and preach the baptism of repentance for the remission of sins." We see here that the Baptist's call to repentance was a necessary preparation for the revelation of the Messiah to Israel. Until Israel had been called back to God in repentance, their long-awaited Messiah could not be revealed among them.

A little further on in the first chapter of Mark, at verses 14 and 15, we read the first message that Christ Himself preached, after John had prepared the way before Him. "Now after that John was put in prison, Jesus came into Galilee, preaching the gospel of the kingdom of God, and saying, The time is fulfilled, and the kingdom of God is at hand: repent ye, and believe the gospel." Here we see that the first commandment that ever fell from the lips of Christ was not to believe, but to repent. First, repent; then believe.

After His death and resurrection, when Christ commissioned His apostles to go out to all nations of the earth with the gospel, once again we find that the first word in His message was "repentance." For we read in Luke's Gospel, chapter 24, verses 46 and 47: "And he said unto them, Thus it is written, and thus it behoved Christ to suffer, and to rise from the dead the third day: and that repentance and remission of sins should be preached in his name among all nations, beginning at Jerusalem." Here again, it is repentance first, and after that remission of sins.

In Acts chapter 2, verses 37 and 38, we read how, shortly afterwards, the apostles, through their spokesman Peter, first began to fulfil this commission of Christ. In verse 37 we read that, after the Holy Spirit's coming on the day of Pentecost, the convicted—but still unconverted—multitude asked: "Men and brethren, what shall we do?" To this inquiry, there came an immediate and definite answer: "Then Peter said unto them, Repent, and be baptized everyone of you in the name of Jesus Christ for the remission of sins, and ye shall receive the gift of the Holy Ghost." Here again, it is repentance first—after that, baptism and remission of sins.

In Acts chapter 20, verses 20 and 21, the apostle Paul himself, speaking to the elders of the church at Ephesus, outlines the gospel message which he had preached to them. He says: "I kept back nothing that was profitable unto you, but have shewed you, and have taught you pubickly, and from house to house, testifying both to the Jews, and also to the Greeks, repentance toward God, and faith toward our Lord Jesus Christ." Once again, the order of Paul's message is the same: first, repentance; then faith.

Finally, as we have already seen, in Hebrews chapter 6, verses 1 and 2, the order of the basic foundation doctrines of the Christian faith is: first, repentance from dead works; then, faith; then, baptisms, and so on.

Without exception, throughout the entire New Testament, repentance is the first response of man to the gospel, demanded by God. Nothing else can come before it, and nothing else can take its place. It is first in order of the six great foundation doctrines enumerated in Hebrews cahpter 6. True repentance must always precede true faith. Without such repentance, faith alone must always be a mere empty profession. This is one main reason why the experience of so many Christians today is so unstable and insecure. They are seeking to build without the first of the great foundation doctrines. They are professing faith but they have never practised true repentance. As a result, the faith which they profess procures for them neither the favour of God, nor the respect of the world. In many places today the simplification of the gospel message has been taken one step too far. The message preached today is: "Only believe." But that is not the message of Christ. Christ and His apostles preached: "Repent, and believe." Any preacher who leaves out the call to repentance is misleading sinners and misrepresenting God. For in Acts chapter 17, verse 30, the apostle Paul tells us that it is God Himself who "now commandeth all men everywhere to repent." That is the general edict of God to the entire human race: "All men **everywhere** must **repent.**"

In Hebrews chapter 6, verse 1, repentance is defined as "repentance from dead works"; and in Acts chapter 20, verse 21, it is defined as "repentance toward God." This means that, in the act of repentance, we turn away from our own dead works and we face toward God, ready to hear and obey the next command which God will then give.

The phrase "dead works" includes all acts and activities of all men that are not based upon repentance and faith. It includes even the acts and activities of religion —even of professing Christianity—if they are not built on this basis. It is in this sense that the prophet Isaiah cries out, in chapter 64, verse 6: "All our righteousnesses are as filthy rags." There is no reference here to acts of open sin and wickedness. Even those acts which are done in the name of religion and morality, if they are not based on true, scriptural repentance and faith, are not acceptable to God. Charity, prayers, church attendance, every kind of religious rite and ordinance—if they are not based on repentance and faith—all alike are merely "dead works" and "filthy rags!"

* * *

There is one further fact about scriptural repentance which must be emphasized. Repentance of this kind is something that begins with God, and not with man. It originates not in the will of man, but in the free and sovereign grace of God. Apart from the working of God's grace and the moving of God's Spirit, man left to himself is incapable of repentance. For this reason the Psalmist cries out three times in Psalm 80, in verse 3, verse 7, and verse 19: "Turn us again, O Lord . . . and we shall be saved." Unless God first moves man toward Himself, man cannot of his own unaided will turn to God and be saved. Likewise, Jeremiah cries out in Lamentations chapter 5, verse 21: "Turn thou us unto thee, O Lord, and we shall be turned." Man cannot turn to God, unless God Himself first moves and draws man. The first move is always with God.

In the New Testament, Christ Himself expressed the same truth, when He said in John's Gospel chapter 6, verse 44: "No man can come to me, except the Father which hath sent me draw him." The first move of the sinner toward God begins with God moving and drawing the sinner to repentance by His Holy Spirit. For this reason, the supreme crisis of every human life comes at the moment of the Spirit's drawing to repentance. Accepted, this drawing leads us to saving faith and eternal life; rejected, it leaves the sinner to continue on his way to the grave and the unending darkness of an eternity apart from God. The scripture makes it plain that even in this life it is possible for a man to pass "the place of repentance"; that is, to get to a place where the Spirit of God will never again draw him to repentance, and where all hope is thus lost even before he actually enters the portals of eternity.

It is fitting to close this study with the words of Christ Himself, in Luke chapter 13, verse 3, and again in verse 5: "Except ye repent, ye shall all likewise perish." Christ was here speaking of men who died in the very act of performing a religious rite; that is, a company of Galileans whose blood Pilate had mingled with their own sacrifices. While actually carrying out their sacrifices in the temple, these men had been executed by order of the Roman Governor, and their own blood had thus been mingled on the temple floor with that of their sacrifices. Yet Christ Himself tells us that these men "perished"; that is, they went to a lost eternity. Even their religious act of sacrifice in the temple could not save their souls, because it was not based on true repentance. The same is true of the religious rites and ordinances and ceremonies of many professing Christians today. None of these religious activities is any substitute for true repentance. Without such repentance, Christ Himself said, "Ye shall all likewise perish."

II
Faith

Bible Definition - Distinguished From Hope - Based Solely On God's Word - Expressed By Confession

Welcome to the Study Hour.

Our textbook—the Bible.

We are continuing today with our series entitled "Foundations." Our study today will be the tenth in this series.

We commenced this series by examining first of all the position of Christ Himself in the Christian faith; and after that, the position of the Bible, as God's Word, in the heart and life of the believer.

In our last study we embarked upon a systematic examination of the six great foundation doctrines of the Christian faith, as stated in the Epistle to the Hebrews, chapter 6, verses 1 and 2. The six doctrines presented to us in these verses as the beginning, or foundation, of the doctrine of Christ are as follows: Number 1, repentance from dead works; Number 2, faith toward God; Number 3, the doctrine of baptisms; Number 4, laying on of hands; Number 5, resurrection of the dead; Number 6, eternal judgment.

In our last study we examined the meaning and the nature of true scriptural repentance. In our present study we shall now go on to examine the second of these great foundation doctrines, called in the Epistle to the Hebrews "faith toward God"—or, more simply, "faith."

Throughout the whole Bible, both Old Testament and New Testament alike, great emphasis is laid on faith, and great importance is attached to it. This indicates that we should be wise to make a careful study of this whole subject of faith.

Earlier in this series, as we studied the effects which God's Word produces in those who receive it, we referred to the statement in Romans chapter 10, verse 17: "So then faith cometh by hearing, and hearing by the word of God." We pointed out that this sets clear and definite limits to the use of the word "faith" in the scriptures. Outside the scriptures, the word "faith" has many wide and different meanings, but in our present study we do not need to concern ourselves with these. Within the scriptures, there are two definite, distinguishing features of faith, as there used. First, such faith always originates directly in God's Word; second, it is always directly related to God's Word.

Faith is one of comparatively few words used in the Bible of which we are there given an actual definition. This scriptural definition of faith is found in Hebrews chapter 11, verse 1: "Now faith is the substance of things hoped for, the evidence of things not seen." This verse might also be translated: "Now faith is the ground, or confidence, of things hoped for, a sure persuasion, or conviction, concerning things not seen."

This important verse brings out various facts about faith. First of all, it indicates a distinction between faith and hope. There are two main ways in which faith differs from hope. The first is that hope is directed toward the future, but faith is established in the present. Hope is an attitude of expectancy concerning things that are still future, but faith is a substance—a confidence—something real and definite within us, that we already possess here and now.

The second main difference between faith and hope is that hope is primarily in the realm of the mind; faith is primarily in the realm of the heart. This is very strikingly brought out in the description of various items of scriptural armour required by the Christian soldier, given to us by the apostle Paul in First Thessalonians chapter 5, verse 8: "But let us, who are of the day, be sober, putting on the breastplate of faith and love; and for an helmet, the hope of salvation." Notice that faith—together with love—is found in the region of the breast—that is, the region of the heart; but hope on the other hand is associated, as a helmet, with the region of the head—that is, the region of the mind. Thus, hope is primarily a mental attitude of expectancy concerning the future; faith is primarily a condition of the heart, producing within us, here and now, something so real that it can be described by the word "substance."

In Romans chapter 10, verse 10, the exercise of faith —or believing—is again directly associated with the heart, for Paul says there: "With the heart man believeth unto righteousness." Many people make a profession of faith in Christ and the Bible, but their faith is only in the realm of the mind, it is a mere intellectual acceptance of certain facts and doctrines. This is not true, scriptural faith, and it does not produce any vital change in the lives of those who profess it. On the other hand, heart faith always produces a definite change, a definite experience, in those who profess it. When associated with the heart, the verb "to believe" becomes a verb of motion. Paul says: "With the heart man believeth **unto** righteousness"—not merely "in righteousness," but "**unto** righteousness." It is one thing to believe with the mind "in righteousness," merely as an abstract theory, or ideal. It is quite another thing to believe with the heart "**unto** righteousness"—that is, to believe in a way that produces a change and a transformation of habits, and character, and life.

In John's Gospel, chapter 6, verse 47, Christ Himself uses the verb "to believe" as a verb of change or of motion. The King James Version of this verse reads, "Verily, verily, I say unto you, He that believeth on me hath everlasting life." The meaning of the preposition "on," when used in connection with the verb "to believe," is not clear. But the normal and literal translation of the preposition here used in the Greek text is not "on," but "into." Literally, therefore, what Christ says is this: "He that believeth **into** me hath everlasting life." This brings out the fact that the verb "to believe" is associated with a process of change, or motion. It is not enough to believe "in" Christ, with mere mental acceptance of the facts of His life, or the truths of His teaching. We must believe "**into**" Christ— we must be moved by heartfelt faith out of ourselves and into Christ, out of our sin and into His righteousness, out of our weakness and into His power, out of our failure and into His victory, out of our limitations and into His omnipotence. This true, scriptural faith of the heart always produces change and transformation. It is always believing **into** Christ and **unto** righteousness; and the result is always something definite, experienced here and now, not something merely hoped for in the future.

For this reason, here in John chapter 6; verse 47, Christ uses the present, and not the future tense. He says: "He that believeth **into** me **hath** everlasting life" —not "shall have," but "hath"—here and now—already "hath" everlasting life. True scriptural faith **into** Christ produces everlasting life here and now within the believer. It is not something that we hope to have in the next world, after death. It is something that we already possess, something that we already enjoy, a reality, a substance, here and now.

So many people have a religion which they hope will somehow do them good in the hour of death, when they reach the threshold of eternity. But true Bible faith gives the believer a here-and-now experience and an assurance of everlasting life already within him. His faith is a real substance within him; and because of this present faith he also has a serene hope, a sure confidence concerning the future. A hope that is based on this present faith will stand the test of death and eternity; but a hope that is not built on this present substance of faith is doomed to final, bitter disillusionment.

* * *

Let us turn back now to the definition of faith given in Hebrews chapter 11, verse 1, and note one further important fact about faith there defined. Faith is "the evidence of things not seen"—or "a sure conviction concerning things not seen." This shows that faith deals with **things not seen.** Faith is not based on the evidence of our physical senses, but on the eternal, invisible truths and realities revealed by God's Word. In Second Corinthians chapter 5, verse 7, Paul brings out this contrast between the objects of faith and the objects of sense perception, for he says: "For we walk by faith, not by sight." "Faith" is here contrasted with "sight." Sight—and the other physical senses—are related to the objects of the physical and material world. Faith is related to the truths revealed in God's Word. Our senses deal with things that are material, temporary, and changeable. Faith deals with the revealed truths of God, which are invisible, eternal, and unchanging.

If we are carnally minded, we can accept only that which our senses reveal to us. But if we are spiritually minded, our faith makes the truths of God's Word more real than anything which our senses may reveal to us. We do not base our faith on that which we see or experience; we base our faith on God's Word. Thereafter, that which we see or experience is the outcome of that which we have already believed. In spiritual experience, sight comes after faith, not before it. In Psalm 27, verse 13, David says: "I had fainted, unless I had believed to see the goodness of the Lord in the land of the living . . ." David did not see first, and then believe. He believed first, and thereafter he saw. Notice also that the experience which faith produced for him was, as we have already emphasized, not merely something after death, in the next world, but here and now, "in the land of the living."

This same lesson is brought out in the conversation between Jesus and Martha outside the tomb of Lazarus, recorded in John's Gospel, chapter 11, verses 39 and 40;

"Jesus said, Take ye away the stone. Martha, the sister of him that was dead, saith unto him, Lord, by this time he stinketh: for he hath been dead four days."

"Jesus saith unto her, Said I not unto thee, that, if thou wouldest believe, thou shouldest see the glory of God?"

Here Jesus makes it plain that faith consists in believing first, then seeing—not in seeing first, then believing. Most carnally-minded people reverse this order. They say: "I only believe in what I can see." But this is incorrect. When we actually see a thing, we do not need to exercise faith for it. It is when we cannot see, that we need to exercise faith. As Paul says, "faith" and "sight" are opposite in their nature.

Quite often in our experience we find that there is an apparent conflict between the evidence of our senses and the revelation of God's Word. For instance, we may see and feel within our bodies all the evidence of physical sickness. Yet the Bible reveals in Matthew chapter 8, verse 17, that Jesus "Himself took our infirmities and bare our sicknesses;" and again in Isaiah chapter 53, verse 5, "With his stripes we are healed." Here is an apparent conflict. Our senses tell us that we are sick. The Bible tells us that we are healed. This conflict between the testimony of our senses and the testimony of God's Word confronts us, as believers, with the possibility of two alternative reactions. On the one hand, we may accept the testimony of our senses, and thus accept our condition of physical sickness. In this way, we become the slaves of our carnal mind. On the other hand, we may hold firmly to the testimony of God's Word, that we are healed. If we do this with persistent, active faith, the testimony of our senses will in due course be brought into line with the testimony of God's Word, and we shall then be able to say that we are healed, not merely on the basis of faith in God's Word, but also on the basis of actual physical experience and of the testimony of our senses.

Herein lies the difference between the carnal mind and the spiritual mind. The carnal mind accepts the testimony of the senses in all circumstances, and is thus ruled by the senses. The spiritual mind accepts the testimony of God's Word as invariably and unchangeably true, and then accepts the testimony of the senses only insofar as it agrees with the testimony of God's Word. Thus, the attitude of the spiritual mind toward the testimony of God's Word is summed up by David in Psalm 119, verse 31: "I have stuck unto—or held onto—thy testimonies: O Lord, put me not to shame." And again in verse 152 of the same Psalm: "Concerning thy testimonies, I have known of old that thou hast founded them forever."

* * *

The outstanding scriptural pattern of this kind of faith that rises above the level of the physical senses to the realm of God's unchanging truth is found in the experience of Abraham, as described by Paul in Romans chapter 4, verses 17 through 21. In verse 17 Paul tells us that

Abraham's faith was directed toward God, "who quickeneth the dead, and calleth those things which be not as though they were." This statement that God "calleth those things which be not as though they were" means that, as soon as God has declared a thing to be true, faith immediately reckons that thing to be true, even though no evidence of its truth may be manifested to the senses. Thus, God called Abraham "a father of many nations," and from that moment forward Abraham immediately began to reckon himself as being what God had called him, "a father of many nations," even though at that time he had not even one son born to Sarah and himself. Abraham did not wait to accept God's statement as true until he saw the evidence of it being worked out in his physical experience. On the contrary, he accepted God's statement as true first, and later, because of this, his physical experience was brought into line with what God had declared.

Then again, in the next verse—Romans chapter 4, verse 18—Paul tells us that Abraham "against hope believed in hope." This phrase "believed in hope" tells us that at this time Abraham had both faith and hope—hope concerning the future, and faith in the present; and that his hope concerning the future was the outcome of his faith in the present.

Again, in the next verse—verse 19—Paul tells us that Abraham "considered not his own body now dead, when he was about an hundred years old, neither yet the deadness of Sarah's womb." This indicates that Abraham refused to accept the testimony of his own senses as to the condition of his own and Sarah's body. The testimony of his senses undoubtedly was that it was no longer possible for either of them to have a child. But Abraham did not accept this testimony because it did not agree with what God had said. On that account, Abraham turned a deaf ear to the testimony of his senses; he refused to consider it.

In the next two verses—verses 20 and 21—Paul goes on to say: "He (Abraham) staggered not at the promise of God through unbelief . . . being fully persuaded that what he (God) had promised, he was able also to perform." This shows us clearly the object upon which Abraham's faith was focused; this was God's promise. Thus, faith is based on the promises and statements of God's Word, and accepts the testimony of the senses only insofar as they agree with the statements of God's Word.

A little earlier—in Romans chapter 4, verse 11—Paul calls Abraham "the father of all them that believe," and in the next verse he speaks of those "who also walk in the steps of that faith of our father Abraham." This shows that true, scriptural faith consists in acting like Abraham and in following the steps of his faith. In analyzing the nature of Abraham's faith, we have seen that there were three successive steps, or stages. First, Abraham accepted God's promise as being true from the moment that it was uttered. Second, Abraham refused to accept the testimony of his senses as long as it did not agree with the statement of God. Third, because Abraham held fast to what God had promised, his physical experience and the testimony of his senses were brought into line with the statement of God. Thus, the thing which he had first accepted in naked faith, contrary to the testimony of his senses, became an actual reality in his own physical experience, confirmed by the testimony of his senses.

By many, this attitude of accepting God's Word as true in defiance of the testimony of our senses would be dismissed as mere foolishness, or fanaticism. Yet the remarkable thing is that philosophers and psychologists of many different ages and backgrounds have agreed in declaring that the testimony of our physical senses is variable, subjective, and unreliable. If, then, the testimony of our senses cannot be accepted, by itself, as true and reliable, where can we find the correct standard of truth and reality, by which the testimony of the senses must be judged? To this question neither philosophy nor psychology has ever been able to offer any satisfactory answer. Indeed, all down the centuries, philosophers and psychologists have echoed the question asked by Pilate as he sat in his judgment hall: "What is truth?" For the Christian believer, however, the answer is found in the words of Christ to His Father, in John chapter 17, verse 17: "Thy word is truth." The ultimate, unchanging standard of all truth and reality is found in God's Word. Faith consists in hearing, believing, and acting upon this truth.

In considering the relationship between faith and our physical senses, it is necessary to make a clear and careful distinction between true, scriptural faith on the one hand, and such teachings as "mind-over-matter," or "Christian Science" (falsely so called) on the other hand. The two main points of difference are as follows: First, teachings such as "mind-over-matter," or "Christian Science," tend to magnify and exalt the purely human element—such things as man's mind, or reason, or will power. Thus, these teachings are essentially man-centred. On the other hand, true, scriptural faith is essentially God-centred. It abases all that is human, and magnifies and exalts only God, and God's truth and power

Secondly, teachings such as "mind-over-matter," or "Christian Science," are not based directly, or even mainly, upon the Word of God. Many of the things which they assert, and which they seek to make real by the exercise of the human will, are not in accordance with the teaching of God's Word. In fact, in certain important respects, they are directly contrary to God's Word. On the other hand, true, scriptural faith, by its very nature and definition, is confined within the limits of God's Word.

* * *

We come now to another important and distinctive feature of true, scriptural faith in man's heart, as it is described for us in the Bible. We have already considered the words of Paul in the first half of Romans chapter 10, verse 10: "With the heart man believeth unto righteousness." In the second half of this verse, Paul adds: "And with the mouth **confession** is made unto salvation." Paul here brings out the direct connection between faith in the heart and confession with the mouth.

This connection between the heart and the mouth is one of the great basic principles of scripture. Christ Himself lays down this principle in Matthew's Gospel chapter 12, verse 34, where He says: "For out of the abundance of the heart the mouth speaketh." We might express this in more modern phraseology by saying: "When the heart is full, it overflows through the mouth." It follows, therefore, that when our heart is full of faith in Christ, this faith will find its proper expression as we confess Christ openly with our mouth. A faith that is held back in silence, without any open confession, is an incomplete faith, which will not bring the results and the blessings that we desire.

In Second Corinthians chapter 4, verse 13, Paul again refers to this connection between believing and speaking, for he says: "We having the same spirit of faith, according as it is written, I believed, and therefore have I spoken; we also believe, and therefore speak." Note the direct and logical connection indicated by the word "therefore": "we also believe, and therefore speak." Paul here speaks about "the spirit of faith." Mere intellectual faith in the mind may perhaps keep silent; but faith that is spiritual—faith that is in the spirit and heart of man—this must speak, this must be expressed in confession with the mouth.

Actually this truth follows logically from the very meaning of the word "confession". The English word "confession"—just like the Greek word "homologia," of which it is a translation—means literally "saying the same as." Thus, confession, for Christians, means that we say the same thing with our mouth, as God Himself has already said in His Word. Or, more briefly, the words of our mouth agree with the Word of God. Thus, confession, in this sense, is the natural expression of heart faith. We believe in our heart what God has said in His Word—this is faith. Thereafter we naturally say the same with our mouth as we believe in our heart—this is confession. Faith and confession centre in one and the same thing—the truth of God's Word.

There are two passages in the Epistle to the Hebrews which further emphasize the importance of confession in relation to faith. In Hebrews chapter 3, verse 1, Christ is called "the High Priest of our profession—or confession" (Both these words are used to translate one and the same word in the original text). This means that Christ in heaven serves as our Advocate and Representative in respect of every truth of God's Word to which we on earth confess with our mouth. But whenever we fail to confess our faith on earth, we give Christ no opportunity to act on our behalf in heaven. By closing our lips on earth, we also close the lips of our Advocate in heaven. The extent of Christ's high-priestly ministry on our behalf in heaven is determined by the extent of our confession on earth.

Again, in Hebrews chapter 10, verse 23, we are told: "Let us hold fast the profession—or confession—of our faith without wavering; (for he is faithful that promised)." Not merely must our faith be without wavering; our confession must also be without wavering. Once we have begun to confess that which we believe, we must continue to confess it boldly and unwaveringly, until that which we have thus believed and confessed has been made real and actual in our experience. True faith must always be expressed through confession, and can never be separated from it.

* * *

Let us now sum up briefly the various facts which we have discovered concerning faith as defined and described in the Bible.

Scriptural faith is a condition of the heart, not the mind. It is in the present, not the future. It produces a positive change in our behaviour and experience. It is based solely on God's Word, and accepts the testimony of the senses only when this agrees with the testimony of God's Word. It is expressed by confession with the mouth.

In our next study in this series we shall continue to examine further aspects of the Bible's teaching concerning faith.

III
Faith

Its Unique And Supreme Importance—The Only Basis Of All Righteous Living—Appropriating All God's Promises.

Welcome to the Study Hour.

Our textbook—the Bible.

The study which we shall now bring to you is the eleventh in our present series, entitled "Foundations."

We are at present engaged in a systematic examination of the six great foundation doctrines of the Christian faith, as stated in the Epistle to the Hebrews, chapter 6, verses 1 and 2. The six doctrines presented to us in these verses as the beginning, or foundation, of the doctrine of Christ are as follows: Number 1, repentance from dead works; Number 2, faith toward God; Number 3, the doctrine of baptisms; Number 4, laying on of hands; Number 5, resurrection of the dead; Number 6, eternal judgment.

In our study last week, we commenced to examine the second of these great foundation doctrines, called in the Epistle to the Hebrews "faith toward God"—or, more simply, "faith."

At the close of last week's study, we made the following brief summary of the main facts which we had discovered concerning faith as defined and described in the Bible:

Scriptural faith is a condition of the heart, not the mind. It is in the present, not the future. It produces a positive change in our behaviour and experience. It is based solely on God's Word, and accepts the testimony of the senses only when this agrees with the testimony of God's Word. It is expressed by confession with the mouth.

In continuing our study of scriptural faith today, it would be wise to consider some of the many scriptures which speak of the unique and supreme importance of faith in man's relationship to God. We have already considered the definition of faith given in the Epistle to the Hebrews chapter 11, verse 1. Five verses further on—that is, in Hebrews chapter 11, verse 6—we find the following statement concerning the part played by faith in man's approach to God: "But without faith it is impossible to please him (that is, God): for he that cometh to God must believe that he is, and that he is a rewarder of them that diligently seek him." Notice the two phrases: "without faith it is impossible to please God"; and again, "he that cometh to God **must believe.**" We see from these that faith is the indispensable condition upon which alone any man at any time can approach God, or please God.

The negative aspect of this truth is stated in the second part of Romans chapter 14, verse 23: "for whatsoever is not of faith is sin." This shows plainly that anything whatever that any person may do at any time, if it is not done in true, scriptural faith, is reckoned by God as sinful. This applies even to religious acts or activities, such as attendance at church, the saying of prayers, or the singing of hymns, or deeds of charity. If these acts are not performed in sincere faith toward God, then they are in no way acceptable to Him. Unless such acts have been preceded by true repentance, and unless they are motivated by true faith, they are nothing but "dead works," totally unacceptable to God.

Perhaps the most all-inclusive statement concerning the relationship between faith and righteousness is found in the prophet Habbakuk, chapter 2, verse 4: "The just shall live by his faith." In considering this and similar passages, it is helpful to remember that the two English words "just" and "righteous" are simply two alternative ways of translating one and the same word in the original text. This applies equally to the Hebrew of the Old Testament and to the Greek of the New Testament. In both languages alike there is only one root word, which as an adjective can be translated either by "just" or by "righteous," and as a noun can be translated either by "justice" or by "righteousness." Whichever translation may be used, there is no difference whatever in the original sense. Thus, in translating Habbakuk chapter 2, verse

4, we may say either, "The just shall live by his faith," or "The righteous shall live by his faith."

This statement of Habakkuk is quoted three times in the New Testament: in Romans chapter 1, verse 17; in Galatians chapter 3, verse 11; and in Hebrews chapter 10, verse 38. In each of these three passages the King James Version renders it: "The just shall live by faith."

It would be difficult to think of any sentence so short and so simple as this, that has produced so great an impact upon the history of the human race. In the King James Version, the entire sentence consists of only six or seven words, none of them containing more than one syllable. Yet this sentence provided the basic, scriptural authority for the gospel message preached by the apostolic church; and the preaching of this simple message by a tiny, despised minority had within three centuries brought to his knees the great imperial Caesar himself—the head of the most powerful, the most far-reaching, and the most long-established empire that the world had ever seeen. About twelve centuries later, this same short, simple sentence, quickened by the Holy Spirit to the heart and mind of Martin Luther, provided the scriptural lever that dislodged the power of papal Rome, and through the Protestant Reformation changed the course of history, first in Europe, and then, by its outreach, in the world at large. There is no doubt that still today, this same short, simple sentence, when once apprehended and applied by faith, contains within itself the power to revolutionize the lives of individuals or the course of nations or empires.

Though so short and so simple, the scope of this sentence, "the just shall live by faith," is immense. The word "live" covers almost every conceivable condition or act of any sentient being. It covers all areas of the total human personality and experience in every conceivable aspect—the spiritual, the mental, the physical, the material. It covers the widest possible range of activities—such as breathing, thinking, speaking, eating, sleeping, working, and so on. The scripture teaches that, for any person to be accepted as righteous by God, all these activities within that person must be motivated and controlled by the one great basic principle of faith.

In Romans chapter 14, verse 23, Paul actually applies this principle to the simple, familiar act of eating, for he says: "And he that doubteth is damned—or condemned—if he eat, because he eateth not of faith: for whatsoever is not of faith is sin." This shows that, in the life of righteousness which alone is acceptable to God, even an act so commonplace as eating food must be performed in faith.

Let us therefore consider for a moment: What does it mean to "eat in faith"? What is implied by this?

We may answer that this implies three main things:

First, it implies that we acknowledge that God is the one who has provided us with the food that we eat. Thus, the provision of nourishing food for our bodies is an example of the principle stated in the Epistle of James, chapter 1, verses 16 and 17: "Do not err, my beloved brethren. Every good gift and every perfect gift is from above, and cometh down from the Father of lights, with whom is no variableness, neither shadow of turning." It is also a fulfilment of the promise contained in Philippians chapter 4, verse 19: "But my God shall supply all your need according to his riches in glory by Christ Jesus."

Second, because we acknowledge that God is the one who provides our food, we naturally pause before eating, to thank Him for it. In this way, we obey the commandment contained in Colossians chapter 3, verse 17: "And whatsoever ye do in word or deed, do all in the name of the Lord Jesus, giving thanks to God and the Father by him." In this way, too, we are assured of God's blessing upon the food that we eat, so that we obtain the maximum amount of nourishment and benefit from it. This is explained by Paul in First Timothy, chapter 4, verses 4 and 5: "For every creature of God is good, and nothing to be refused, if it be received with thanksgiving: for it is sanctified by the word of God and prayer." Thus, through our faith and prayer, the food that we eat is blessed and sanctified to us.

Thirdly, eating in faith implies that we acknowledge that the health and strength we receive through our food belong to God and must be used in His service and for

His glory. We hereby acknowledge the principle stated by Paul in First Corinthians, chapter 6, verse 13: "Now the body is not for fornication"—not for any immoral, unclean, foolish, or harmful use—"but for the Lord; and the Lord for the body." Because our bodies are thus by faith and by holy living given over to the Lord, the responsibility for their care and preservation also belongs to the Lord; and we have every right to expect the fulfillment of the apostle Paul's prayer in First Thessalonians chapter 5, verse 23: "And I pray God your whole spirit and soul and body be preserved blameless unto the coming of our Lord Jesus Christ."

All these—and many more besides—are the implications and the outworkings of the principle, "The just shall live by faith, as applied to one simple aspect only of our lives—that of eating. And when we thus analyze what is implied by the phrase, "to eat in faith," we are forced to the conclusion that the great majority of people in North America today—even of those who profess Christianity—do not "eat in faith." In the provision, the preparation, and the consumption of their daily food no thought whatever is given to God. No doubt, here is one main cause of the appalling increase of such diseases as indigestion, ulcers, tumors, arthritis, and many others. In spite of an unprecedented abundance of both food and money, countless thousands are misusing and abusing this abundance to their own great physical distress, because by their indifference and unbelief they have shut God out of their lives. In Ecclesiastes chapter 5, verse 17, Solomon gives us a picture of the carnal, sensual man who makes no room for God in his daily life: "All his days also he **eateth in darkness**, and he hath much **sorrow** and **wrath** with his **sickness**." This description is still as true today as when Solomon wrote it. Not to eat in faith is to eat in "darkness," and three consequences that commonly follow this are "sorrow," "wrath," and "sickness."

* * *

There is another simple act, familiar to us all, and essential to all living, in which the principle of faith can have a decisive influence—and that is the act of sleeping. In Psalm 127, verse 2, the Psalmist says: "It is vain for you to rise up early, to sit up late, to eat the bread of sorrows: for so he (God) giveth his beloved sleep." Through the continual, restless pursuit of wealth and pleasure, millions today are losing the ability to enjoy either food or sleep. Who can count the millions of pain killers, of digestive tablets, and of sleeping tablets, that are consumed each day across the North American continent— and often with so little effect? But to God's believing children, to those whose lives are based on faith in God, sleep comes as a gift of God's love, a provision of His daily mercy—"for so he **giveth** his beloved **sleep.**" Someone has said: "Money can buy medicine, but not health; a bed, but not sleep." It is not only very costly, but it is also very injurious to our bodies, to shut God out of our daily living.

The Psalmist David was a man whose way led through many troubles and dangers, but in the midst of them all his faith in God sustained him and gave him the assurance of sweet, untroubled rest and sleep. Listen to David's own testimony of what prayer and faith could do for him. In Psalm 3, verses 4 and 5, he says: "I cried unto the Lord with my voice, and he heard me out of his holy hill. I laid me down and slept; I awaked; for the Lord sustained me." Again in Psalm 4, verse 8, he says: "I will both lay me down in peace, and sleep: for thou, Lord, only makest me dwell in safety." This same blessed assurance of calm, untroubled sleep at the close of each day is still available to those who will enter into all the provisions of God's love and mercy contained in that simple phrase: "The just shall live by faith."

* * *

At this point, I can hear someone say: "You have spoken about simple, familiar acts such as eating and sleeping, and the part that faith can play in these. But the problems of our modern world are much greater and more complex than simple things like eating and sleeping. What solution can faith offer to our great national and international problems today?"

Yes, it is certainly true that we are confronted in the world today with vast and intricate problems—social, economic, political. We must acknowledge this. But let us take the truth one step further: There is no human mind and there is no human wisdom that can even comprehend all these problems in their entirety, much less work out solutions to them all. If we must depend solely upon human wisdom for the solutions, then the outlook is hopeless. But faith does not need to take this hopeless attitude. True faith is always united with humility. True faith causes man to acknowledge his own limitations. True faith distinguishes between those things which are within the province of man, and those which are within the province of God. Someone has stated the relationship between man's part and God's part in the life of faith, as follows: "You do the simple thing; God will do the complicated thing. You do the small thing; God will do the great thing. You do the possible thing; God will do the impossible thing."

God's simple plan for living, "The just shall live by faith," still makes sense today. Let man do his part—let man by faith and obedience seek God's guidance and blessing in the simple acts of daily life, in the familiar relationships of home and community. There will come a relief and a release from the strains, the tensions, the physical, mental and moral breakdown of modern life. And in the vast areas of the modern world that are outside man's comprehension and control, God will move in response to man's faith and will overrule the affairs of nations in a way that will amaze us by its effectiveness. This simple principle, "The just shall live by faith," which has twice changed the course of world history, still contains today the power to revolutionize the life and destiny of any modern nation that will apply it. This is still God's answer to man's problems, God's provision for man's needs: "The just shall live by faith." Of all man's faculties and capacities, there is only one by which he can solve the problems which confront him today—one human faculty which is potentially greater than all his material and scientific achievements, and that is: man's faith in God.

In order to comprehend to the full the possibilities latent in man's faith in God, it is necessary to set side by side two statements made by the Lord Jesus Christ during His earthly ministry. In Matthew chapter 19, verse 26, we read: "But Jesus beheld them, and said unto them, With men this is impossible; but with God all things are possible." In Mark chapter 9, verse 23, we read: "Jesus said unto him, If thou canst believe, all things are possible to him that believeth." Set these two statements side by side: "**With God** all things are possible," and "All things are possible **to him that believeth.**" This means that through faith God's possibilities become ours. Faith is the channel by which God's omnipotence becomes available to man. The limit of what faith can receive is the limit only of what God Himself can do.

* * *

There is time in our study today to consider just one more aspect of this great subject of faith. We have spoken hitherto of faith as an experience of the human heart, which revolutionizes human behaviour and provides a principle by which to direct the whole course of human life. However, it is most important to add that faith is not merely something subjective, something private and personal in the heart of each believer. It is this, but it is also more. Faith is based on definite, objective facts. We may ask: What are these facts upon which faith is based? It is possible to give a very wide answer to this question. On the other hand, it is possible also to confine our answer within quite narrow limits.

In the widest sense, faith is based upon the entire Bible. Every statement and every promise in the whole Bible is a potential object of faith. As we have already said, faith comes through hearing the Word of God; and faith is therefore based upon everything that God's Word contains. For the Christian believer in this dispensation, there is nothing within the statements and promises of God that is outside the scope of his faith. This is plainly stated by the apostle Paul in Second Corinthians chapter 1, verse 20, where he says: "For all the promises of God in him (that is, Christ) are yea, and in him Amen, unto the glory of God **by us.**" Side by side with this we may set also Romans chapter 8, verse 32: "He that spared not his own Son, but delivered him up for us all, how shall he not with him also freely give us **all things**?" All things that God possesses—all His blessings—all His promises —all are made freely available to each person who will receive them through faith in Christ's atoning death and resurrection.

There is a tendency in some quarters today to base the interpretation of scripture on a system of dispensations in such a way that only a small proportion of God's blessings and promises are made available to Christian believers in the present age. According to this system of interpretation, many of God's choicest blessings and promises are relegated either to periods in the past, such as that of the Mosaic Covenant, or the apostolic church, or to periods in the future, such as the millennium, or the dispensation of the fulness of times. However, this does not tally with Paul's statement in Second Corinthians, chapter 1, verse 20, where he says: "For all the promises of God—not some of the promises of God, but all the promises of God—in him (Christ) **are**—not were nor will be—but are here and now—yea and Amen—not merely yea—not merely a simple affirmative—but yea and Amen— a double affirmative—unto the glory of God **by us**—not by various groups in different ages—but by us"—where the whole context makes it plain that "us" includes, without any qualification, all true Christian believers.

There is no need in the life of any Christian believer which is outside the scope of God's promises. Paul makes this plain in Philippians chapter 4, verse 19, where he says: "But my God shall supply all your need according to his riches in glory by Christ Jesus." For every need that can arise in the life of any Christian there is somewhere in God's Word a promise that meets that need and may be claimed through faith in Christ. Thus, whenever a need arises in the life of a Christian, there are three simple steps that he must take: First, he must locate in God's Word the promise that fits his need; second, he must obediently fulfil in his life the particular conditions attached to that promise; third, he must firmly and positively claim the fulfilment of the promise. This is faith in action; and faith of this kind, the apostle John tells us in his First Epistle chapter 5, verse 4, is "the victory that overcometh the world." It will be seen that the secret of this victory lies in knowing and applying the promises of God's Word.

The apostle Peter states this same truth most clearly and definitely in his Second Epistle chapter 1, verses 3 and 4, where he tells us that God's "divine power hath given unto us **all things** that pertain unto life and godliness, through the knowledge of him (that is, Christ) who hath called us to glory and virtue; whereby are given unto us **exceeding great and precious promises.**" Here Peter's message is in perfect agreement with that of Paul. He tells us that God has already provided us with all that we can ever need for life and godliness; and that this provision is made available through Christ by the claiming of God's exceeding great and precious promises.

In the Old Testament, under Joshua, God brought His people into a promised land. In the New Testament, under Jesus, God brings His people into a land of promises. In the Old Testament God showed Joshua the principle of active, personal, appropriating faith, for He said in Joshua chapter 1, verse 3: "Every place that the sole of your foot shall tread upon, that have I given unto you." In the New Testament this principle remains the same. God says, in effect: "Every promise that you personally shall claim, that have I given unto you."

However, it is necessary to add one word of warning: the great majority of God's promises, in Old and New Testament alike, are conditional. That is to say, there are conditions attached, which must be fulfilled, before the promise can be claimed. For example, in Psalm 37, verse 5, God says: "Commit thy way unto the Lord; trust also in him; and he shall bring it to pass." The promise here is: "And he shall bring it to pass"—that is, "He shall work out the way of the believer for him." The two conditions which are stated first are: "Commit thy way" and "trust also in him." The word "commit" denotes a single definite act; the word "trust" denotes a continuing attitude. Thus, the conditions attached to this promise may be interpreted as follows: First, make a single, definite act of commitment; second, thereafter maintain a continuing attitude of trust. When these two conditions have been fulfilled, the believer can then claim the ensuing promise, "He shall bring it to pass," in whatever way is needed to meet his own particular situation.

Thus, active, appropriating faith is the key to victorious Christian living. It must be based on the promises of God's Word, and it must follow the three successive steps: First, find the appropriate promise; second, fulfil all the conditions attached; third, claim the fulfilment of the promise. Subject to these conditions, the scope of the Christian's faith is as wide as the promises of God.

IV
Faith For Salvation

The Four Basic Facts Of The Gospel—The Simple Act Of Appropriation.

Welcome to the Study Hour.

Our textbook—the Bible.

The study which we shall now bring you is the twelfth in our present series, entitled "Foundations."

We are at present engaged in a systematic examination of the six great foundation doctrines of the Christian faith, as stated in the Epistle to the Hebrews, chaper 6, verses 1 and 2. The six doctrines presented to us in these verses as the beginning, or foundation, of the doctrine of Christ are as follows: Number 1, repentance from dead works; Number 2, faith toward God; Number 3, the doctrine of baptisms; Number 4, laying on of hands; Number 5, resurrection of the dead; Number 6, eternal judgment.

In our last two studies we have been examining the second of these great foundation doctrines, called in the Epistle to the Hebrews "faith twoard God," or, more simply, "faith." In these two studies we have reached the following conclusions concerning faith as defined and described in the Bible:

Scriptural faith is a condition of the heart, not the mind. It is in the present, not the future. It produces a positive change in our behaviour and experience. It is based solely on God's Word, and accepts the testimony of the senses only when this agrees with the testimony of God's Word. It is expressed by confession with the mouth.

Faith of this kind is the only basis of righteousness acceptable to God, and it must direct and control the entire course of the believer's life.

page forty

Faith is not merely an inward, personal experience, but is based objectively on the revealed facts of God's Word.

Through faith in Christ we are entitled to claim all the promises of God in the Bible. In claiming any of these promises there are three steps that we must follow: first, locate the promise that fits our particular need; second, meet all the conditions attached to that particular promise; third, claim the fulfilment of the promise by positive, active faith.

* * *

So far we have considered faith in the widest and most general sense, as related to all the statements and promises of God contained in the entire Bible. However, there is one part of the Bible's message which is of the greatest and most urgent importance, because of the fact that it decides the eternal destiny of every human soul. That is the part of the Bible which we usually call "the gospel," and which reveals the way of salvation for the soul from sin and its consequences.

Very often when people speak of "the gospel," they have in mind something of a vague and emotional nature, which they feel it would be impossible to define or explain in a plain or rational way. Even in the preaching of "the gospel" there is often so much emphasis on an emotional response that the impression is created that the whole of salvation consists in an emotional experience. Yet this is completely incorrect, and gravely misleading. The actual gospel message, as stated in the Bible, consists of certain definite, simple facts; and salvation consists in knowing, believing and applying these facts.

What are these facts which constitute the gospel?

For an answer to this question we may turn to two passages in the writings of the apostle Paul. These two passages are: Romans chapter 4, verses 24 and 25; and First Corinthians chapter 15, verses 1 through 4.

In Romans chapter 4, Paul analyzes the main features of the faith of Abraham, and sets forth Abraham's faith as an example to be followed by all Christian believers. He points out that, according to the Old Testament scriptures, Abraham was not justified before God by his works, but that his faith was imputed to him for righteousness. Then in the last three verses of the chapter—verses 23, 24 and 25—Paul directly applies this example of Abraham to us as believers in Christ, for he says:

"Now it was not written for his sake alone, that it was imputed to him;

"But for us also, to whom it shall be imputed; if we believe on him that raised up Jesus our Lord from the dead;

"Who was delivered for our offences, and was raised again for our justification."

The gospel, as here stated by Paul, contains three definite facts: first, Jesus was delivered to the punishment of death for our offences; second, God raised Jesus up again from the dead; third, if we believe this record of the death and resurrection of Jesus on our behalf, we shall be justified, or accepted as righteous, before God.

In First Corinthians chapter 15, verses 1 through 4, Paul reminds the Christians at Corinth of the gospel message which he had preached to them and through which they had been saved, and he again sets forth for them the basic facts of the message:

"Moreover, brethren, I declare unto you the gospel which I preached unto you, which also ye have received, and wherein ye stand;

"By which also ye are saved, if ye keep in memory—or hold fast—what I preached unto you, unless ye have believed in vain.

"For I delivered unto you first of all that which I also received, how that Christ died for our sins according to the scriptures;

"And that he was buried, and that he rose again the third day according to the scriptures . . ."

Again we see that the gospel, as here stated by Paul, consists of three simple, definite facts: first, Christ died for our sins; second, He was buried; third, He rose again the third day. Paul also emphasizes that the first and most authoritative of all testimonies to the truth of these facts is not the testimony of the men who were eye-witnesses of Christ's death and resurrection, but the testimony of the Old Testament scriptures, which had prophetically foreshown these events hundreds of years before they actually took place. The testimony of contemporary eye-witnesses is only mentioned later, as supporting that of the Old Testament Scriptures.

If we set side by side the teaching of these two passages from Paul's Epistles which we have considered—Romans chapter 4, verses 24 and 25, and First Corinthians chapter 15, verses 1 through 4—it is possible to set out in a clear and simple way the basic facts which constitute the gospel. These facts all centre exclusively in the person of Christ Himself—not in His earthly life and teaching—but in His death and resurrection. We may say that there are four basic facts: First, Christ was delivered by God the Father to the punishment of death on account of our sins; second, Christ was buried; third, God raised Him from the dead the third day; fourth, righteousness is received from God through believing these facts.

* * *

At this point it is necessary to emphasize once again what we said at the beginning of our first study on "faith" —that there is a vital difference between faith in the mind, which is nothing more than the intellectual acceptance of the facts of the gospel, and faith in the heart, which always results in a definite, positive response to the facts. The whole New Testament makes it plain that the experience of salvation comes to each soul only as a result of this personal response to the gospel.

Various different words are used in the New Testament to describe this active personal response to the gospel. All the words thus used have one essential point in common: they all denote simple, familiar acts, such as anybody can understand and anybody can carry out.

For example, in Romans chapter 10, verses 8 and 9, Paul first explains that salvation comes through believing with the heart, and confessing with the mouth, the truth of the gospel. Then in the same chapter, verse 13, he concludes his explanation of the way of salvation by saying: "For whosoever shall **call** upon the name of the Lord shall be saved." Here the simple act which brings with it the experience of salvation is that of **calling** upon the name of the Lord—that is, asking God out loud for salvation in the name of the Lord Jesus Christ.

In Matthew chapter 11, verse 28, Christ uses the simple, familiar word "**come**" to describe the response which He requires to the gospel invitation, for He says: "**Come** unto me, all ye that labour and are heavy laden, and I will give you rest." In John chapter 6, verse 37, Christ adds to this invitation to come to Him a very gracious and assuring promise: "Him that cometh to me I will in no wise cast out." Thus, the invitation is supported by the promise; and the promise creates the required faith in those who desire to accept the invitation.

In John chapter 4, verse 14, speaking to the Samaritan woman at Jacob's well, Christ uses the simple act of **drinking**, which was appropriate to that particular situation, to express the necessary response to the gospel. He says: "Whosoever **drinketh** of the water that I shall give him shall never thirst; but the water that I shall give him shall be in him a well of water springing up into everlasting life." Here the act of receiving salvation is compared to that of **drinking water.** In this instance, the promise is given first—"he shall never thirst"; then later in the New Testament the promise is supported by an invitation. For in John chapter 7, verse 37, Christ say: "If any man thirst, let him come unto me, and drink." And again, in Revelation chapter 22, verse 17, we read: "And the Spirit and the bride say, Come. And let him that heareth say, Come. And let him that is athirst come. And whosoever will, let him take the water of life freely."

In John chapter 1, verses 11, 12 and 13, the word used by the apostle John to denote this active response to the gospel is the word "**receive**." In these three verses John writes, concerning Christ:

page forty-four

"He came unto his own, and his own received him not.

"But as many as **received** him, to them gave he power to become the sons of God, even to them that believe on his name:

"Which—or who—were born, not of blood, nor of the will of the flesh, nor of the will of man, but of God."

Here the key thought is that of personally "receiving" Christ. The result of this response of faith is here described by John as "becoming a son of God," or "being born of God." Christ himself refers to the same experience in John chapter 3, verse 3, where he calls it being "born again." He there makes it plain that without this definite, personal experience no person can ever hope to enter heaven, for He says: "Verily, verily, I say unto thee, Except a man be born again, he cannot see the kingdom of God."

Once again, this challenge to respond to the gospel by personally receiving Christ, given in John's gospel, is supported by a definite promise given by Christ Himself in Revelation chapter 3, verse 20, where He says: "Behold, I stand at the door, and knock: if any man hear my voice, and open the door, I will come in to him, and will sup with him." Here Christ speaks directly to each individual soul that has heard the gospel and desires to respond by opening the heart's door and receiving Christ thereat. To each soul that will make this response, Christ gives a clear, straightforward promise: "I will come in."

We have seen that in each case where the gospel is presented, faith is required to make a simple, personal response. The word used to describe this response may vary, but the essential nature of the response is always the same. In the cases which we have considered, the following words are used to describe this response: to "call"; to "come"; to "drink"; to "receive." As we have pointed out, each of these denotes a simple, familiar act, such as anybody can understand and anybody can carry out. There is one other vitally important feature which is common to all these acts: each of them is an act that the person concerned **must do for himself**; no one can perform any of these acts on behalf of another person. Each person must "**call**" for himself; each person must "**come**" for himself; each person must "**drink**" for himself; each person must "**receive**" for himself. So it is with the response to the gospel. Each person must make his own response; no person can make the response required from another. Each person will be either saved or lost solely by his own response.

* * *

It is the duty of every responsible Christian—whether minister or layman—to be thoroughly acquainted with these simple basic facts of the gospel, which we have just outlined, and also with the various ways in which the New Testament presents the need for a definite, personal response to the gospel from each soul. The work of Christ's kingdom would be greatly benefited if every minister would make a solemn resolve never to preach a sermon in which these facts of the gospel are not stated clearly at least once. Where sermons are regularly preached without the clear presentation of these facts, it is very questionable whether anything of eternal value will result from such preaching.

I never mention this point without recalling to mind an incident that took place in my own experience while I was working as a minister in London, England. The incident concerns a lady whom we may call "Mrs. H."

Mrs. H. had been coming regularly to our house for some weeks, to give piano lessons to our two young daughters. We did not know much about Mrs. H. except that she was a respectable, good-living woman who regularly attended a well-known Protestant church quite near our home. She gave us to understand that she took some active part in connection with the women's missionary organization in the church.

One day we learned that Mrs. H. had been rushed to the hospital, gravely ill, and was scarcely expected to live. In the circumstances, I felt it my duty to visit her in the hospital. When I asked permission to see her, the nurse replied that she was too ill to have any visitors. When I explained that I was a minister, the nurse told me that I could see her for five minutes—and not a moment longer.

By the time I had introduced myself to Mrs. H. and made sure that she knew who I was, almost one minute of the five had already gone. Without further ado, I told her that she might well be on the threshold of eternity, and asked whether, in such a condition, she had the assurance that her sins were forgiven and that she was ready to meet God. She replied that she did not.

I then told her very clearly and simply the basic facts of the gospel: that Christ suffered death as the punishment for our sins; that He was buried; and rose again the third day; that we may be saved through believing these facts, but that God expects a definite, personal response of faith from each person who desires to be saved.

I asked her if she wished to make this response, and she said that she did.

I asked Mrs. H. to follow me in prayer, and I said out loud a prayer of a few short sentences, repeating the facts of the gospel, and claiming God's promise of salvation. Mrs. H. repreated each sentence after me.

I then asked her if she now believed that she was saved, and she said "Yes."

I concluded by another short prayer, committing her to the Lord, and thanking Him for her salvation.

By this time I still had about half a minute of the five minutes left. Thus, from the moment that I began to deal with Mrs. H. about her soul, it took me less than four minutes to present the gospel to her and to lead her into a definite experience and assurance of salvation.

In this way, Mrs. H. obtained peace in her heart which she had never known in all her previous life, and as a direct consequence of obtaining peace in her heart, she made a most rapid and unexpected recovery from her condition of physical sickness, and was soon discharged from the hospital.

A few weeks later, Mrs. H. was back at our house again, to resume her piano lessons. When the lessons were over, I said: "Do you mind if I ask you a personal question?" She gave her consent.

I then continued: "Mrs. H., I understand that for many years you have faithfully attended your church every week, and have even taken an active part in the life of the church. Yet, when the moment of crisis came, and you found yourself face to face with eternity, you were not at all ready to die or to face God. Do you mind my asking: What kind of subjects does your minister preach about each Sunday?"

"Well," she replied, "he usually preaches about the Christian life and growing in grace."

"But," I replied, "it was no use whatever preaching to you about leading the Christian life or growing in grace, because you had never been born again, and so it was quite impossible for you to lead the Christian life or grow in grace. It is impossible for a baby to start growing up before it has ever been born."

"Yes," she replied, "I realize now that that is true. I'm going to speak to my minister about it."

I could not help wondering what would be the outcome of that. However, she was obviously determined, and I saw no reason to dissuade her.

When I saw Mrs. H. again next week, I said: "Well, did you speak to your minister?"

"Yes, I did," she replied.

"And what did he preach about last Sunday?" I asked.

"He preached that the most important thing is **to know that you are saved.**"

Oh! If only these words could be printed across the top of every program and every bulletin of every church professing the Christian faith: "The most important thing is to know that you are saved."

Imagine that this woman, Mrs. H., had regularly attended a Christian church, several times a week, for many years, and had never come to understand the simple, essential facts upon which the gospel is based, nor the personal response which she herself had to make to the gospel in order to receive the experience of salvation. And yet, in a moment of crisis, it proved possible, within a space of less than four minutes, to present these facts to her in such a way that she made the necessary response and entered into a definite experience and assurance of salvation. How much misused time and misapplied effort must lie behind such a story as this! And yet, doubtless, a case such as this could be multiplied millions of times over in professing Christian churches right around the world.

Once in East Africa I heard a young African evangelist speaking to a white missionary who was responsible for the direction of a group of churches stretching over a wide area; and he made the following statement: "Your churches are only storehouses, storing people for hell." To some people this might appear a shocking statement, especially coming from a black man to a white, and from a national to a missionary. Yet, knowing the situation as I did, I realized that the young African was speaking the truth. The great majority of the members of those churches had never once had the basic facts of the gospel presented to them, and had never been faced with the need to make a definite, personal response to those facts. They had exchanged paganism for a form of Christianity; they had memorized a catechism; they had been through a form of baptism; they had deen accepted as church members; many of them had been educated in mission schools—yet of the essential facts of the gospel and of the experience of salvation, of these they had no knowledge nor understanding whatever. Churches such as these—whether in Africa, or in America, or anywhere else in the world—are just what that young African called them—"storehouses storing people for hell."

The supreme purpose of every true Christian Church, the chief duty of every Christian minister, the main responsibility of every Christian layman is to present to all who may be reached, in the clearest and most forceful way, the basic facts of the gospel of Christ, and to urge all who hear to make the definite, personal response to these facts which God requires. To this, the supreme task, every other duty and activity of the church must be secondary and subsidiary.

* * *

In closing our study today, I want to state once again, with all possible clarity and emphasis, these basic facts of the gospel and the response which each person is required to make.

The basic facts are these: First, Christ was delivered by God the Father to the punishment of death on account of our sins; second, Christ was buried; third, God raised Him from the dead the third day; fourth, righteousness is received from God through believing these facts.

In order to receive salvation, each individual soul must make a direct personal response to Christ. This response can be described in any of the following ways: calling upon the name of Christ, as Lord; coming to Christ; receiving Christ; drinking of the water of life which Christ alone can give.

To every person who has followed our study today I would ask this question: Have you believed these facts? Have you made this definite, personal response?

If not, I urge you to do it now. Pray with me, just as Mrs. H. prayed there with me in that hospital room. Say these words after me now, in prayer:

"Lord Jesus Christ, I believe that you died for my sins; that you were buried; that you rose again the third day. I now repent of my sins.

"I call upon you—I come to you—I receive you—I take from you just now the water of life freely.

"In Jesus' Name, Amen."

V
Faith And Works

Salvation By Faith Alone—Living Faith Always Expressed And Developed By Works

Welcome to the Study Hour.

Our textbook—the Bible.

The study which we shall now bring you is No. 13 in our present series, entitled "Foundations."

We are at present engaged in a systematic examination of the six great foundation doctrines of the Christian faith, as stated in the Epistle to the Hebrews, chapter 6, verses 1 and 2. The six doctrines presented to us in these verses as the beginning, or foundation, of the doctrine of Christ are as follows: Number 1, repentance from dead works; Number 2, faith toward God; Number 3, the doctrine of baptisms; Number 4, laying on of hands; Number 5, resurrection of the dead; Number 6, eternal judgment.

In our last three studies we have been examining the second of these great foundation doctrines, called in the Epistle to the Hebrews "faith toward God"—or, more simply, "faith." We have examined in succession the definition of faith, the nature of faith, the objects of faith, the expression of faith, the relationship of faith to the entire course of the believer's life, and the facts upon which faith is based.

In our study today we shall examine the relation between **faith and works**. This is an important subject, which is referred to in many different passages of the New Testament. Yet it is one about which remarkably little teaching is given in most Christian circles today. As a result, a good many Christians today are left in a condition of confusion or partial bondage, halfway between law and grace. Not a few Christians also, through ignorance on this point, are led astray into false teachings which lay unscriptural emphasis on the observance of some particular day, or the eating of certain special foods, or other similar matters of the law.

It will be helpful to begin our examination of this subject by a few simple words of explanation. What exactly do we mean by "faith," or by "works"? The answer quite simply is that by "faith" we mean "that which we believe," and by "works" we mean "that which we do."

Thus we can express the relationship between faith and works, as taught in the New Testament, by the following simple contrast: Faith is not based on works, but works are the outcome of faith. Or, in still simpler words: What we believe is not based on what we do, but what we do is the outcome of what we believe.

* * *

Let us begin by considering the first part of this statement: Faith is not based on works; or, what we believe is not based on what we do. The whole of the New Testament bears consistent testimony to this vital truth.

In John's Gospel, chapter 19, verse 30, we read this account of the final moments of the sufferings of Jesus upon the cross: "When Jesus therefore had received the vinegar, he said, It is finished: and he bowed his head, and gave up the ghost."

The Greek word here translated "It is finished" is the most emphatic word that could possibly be used. It is the perfect tense of a verb which itself means to do a thing perfectly. We might perhaps bring this out by translating: "It is perfectly perfect." In other words, there remains nothing more whatever to do. All that ever needed to be done to pay the penalty of men's sins and to purchase pardon and salvation for all men has already been accomplished by the sufferings and death of Christ upon the cross. To suggest that any man might ever need to do anything more than Christ has already done to purchase salvation would be to reject the testimony of God's Word and to discredit the efficacy of Christ's atonement. Thus, any attempt by any man thereafter to earn salvation, either wholly or in part, by his own good works is in effect an insult both to God the Father and to God the

Son. It carries the implication that the work of atonement and salvation, planned by the Father and carried out by the Son, is in some sense inadequate or incomplete. This is contrary to the unanimous testimony of the entire New Testament.

This fact that nothing more can ever be done by any man to earn salvation is continually and emphatically taught by the apostle Paul.

For example, in Romans chapter 4, verses 4 and 5, Paul says this: "Now to him that worketh is the reward not reckoned of grace, but of debt. But to him that worketh not, but believeth on him that justifieth the ungodly, his faith is counted for righteousness." Notice the phrase "to him **that worketh not, but believeth.**" In order to obtain salvation by faith, the first thing that any man must do is "**not to work**"—to stop working—to stop trying to do anything whatever to earn salvation. Salvation comes through faith alone, through doing nothing whatever but believing. So long as a man tries to do anything whatever to earn salvation, he cannot experience the salvation of God, which is received by faith alone.

This was the great mistake which Israel made, as Paul—himself an Israelite—explains. For he says in Romans chapter 9, verses 31 and 32: "But Israel, which followed after the law of righteousness, hath not attained to the law of righteousness. Wherefore? Because they sought it not by faith, but as it were by the works of the law." Again in Romans chapter 10, verse 3, Paul says concerning Israel: "For they being ignorant of God's righteousness, and going about to establish their own righteousness, have not submitted themselves unto the righteousness of God." Why did Israel fail to obtain the salvation which God had prepared for them? Paul gives two reasons, which go very closely together: First, "because they sought it not by faith, but as it were by the works of the law"; and second, because they "went about to establish their own righteousness." In other words, they tried to earn salvation by something which they themselves did in their own righteousness. As a result, they never entered into God's salvation.

The same mistake, which was made by Israel in Paul's day, is being made today by many millions of professing Christians right around the world. There are many millions of sincere, well-meaning people in Christian churches everywhere who feel that they must do something to help to earn their salvation. They devote themselves to such things as prayer, penance, fasting, charity, self-denial, the careful observance of church ordinances, but all in vain! They never obtain true peace of heart and assurance of salvation, because—like Israel of old—they seek it not by faith, but by works. They go about to establish their own righteousness, and in this way they fail to submit themselves to the righteousness of God, which is by faith in Christ alone.

Paul teaches the same truth very clearly in Ephesians chapter 2, verses 8 and 9, where he says to the Christian believers: "For by grace are ye saved through faith; and that not of yourselves: it is the gift of God: not of works, lest any man should boast."

Notice that Paul says: "Ye are"—already—"saved." This proves that it is possible to be saved here and now, in this world, and to know it. Salvation is not something for which we have to wait until the next life. We can be saved here and now.

How can his present assurance of salvation be received? It is the gift of God's grace--that is, God's free, unmerited favour towards the sinful and undeserving. This gift is received simply and solely through faith—"not of works, lest any man should boast." If a man could do anything whatever to earn his own salvation, then he could boast of that which he himself had done. He would not owe his salvation entirely to God, but would owe it, in part at least, to his own good works, his own efforts. But when a man receives salvation as a free gift of God, simply through faith, then he has nothing whatever to boast of.

Paul emphasizes this again, in Romans chapter 3, verses 27 and 28: "Where is boasting then? It is excluded. By what law? of works? Nay: but by the law of faith. Therefore we conclude that a man is justified by faith without the deeds of the law."

In Romans chapter 6, verse 23, Paul again presents the total contrast between that which we earn by our works and that which we receive solely by faith, for he says: "For the **wages** of sin is death; but the **gift** of God is eternal life through Jesus Christ our Lord." There is a deliberate contrast between the two words "wages" and "gift." "Wages" denotes that which we have earned by that which we have done. On the other hand, the word translated "gift"—in Greek "charisma"—is directly related to the Greek word for "grace"—"charis." Hence, the word denotes explicitly a free, unmerited gift of God's grace, or favour. Thus, each of us is confronted with a choice. On the one hand, we may choose to take our "wages"— that is, the due reward for our works. But because our own works are sinful and unpleasing to God, the "wages" due to us for them is "death"—not merely physical death, but also final, eternal banishment from the presence of God. On the other hand, we may choose to receive by faith God's free "gift." This "gift" is eternal life, and it is in Jesus Christ. That is to say, when we receive Jesus Christ as our personal Saviour, in Him we receive the gift of eternal life.

The same contrast is presented again by Paul in the Epistle to Titus, chapter 3, verse 5: "Not by works of righteousness which we have done, but according to his mercy he (God) saved us, by the washing of regeneration, and renewing of the Holy Ghost." Nothing could be plainer than this: "not by works of righteousness which we have done, but according to his mercy he saved us." If we desire salvation, it cannot be upon the basis of any works of righteousness which we have done, but simply and solely upon the basis of God's mercy. Our own works must be first excluded, in order that we may receive God's mercy in salvation.

In the second part of this same verse Paul tells us four positive facts about the way God's salvation works in our lives. First, it is a "washing"—that is, we are cleansed from all our sin. Second, it is a "regeneration"—

that is, we are born again, we become children of God. Third, it is a "renewing"—that is, we are made new creatures in Christ. Fourth, it is "of the Holy Ghost"—that is, it is a work of God's own Spirit within our hearts and lives. None of this can in any way at all be the result of our own works, but all of it is received simply and solely through faith in Christ.

If salvation is not at all by works, but solely by faith, we may naturally ask: "What part then do works play in the life of the Christian believer?" The fullest and clearest answer to this question in the New Testament is given by James in his Epistle, chapter 2, verses 14 through 26. This is what he says:

> "What doth it profit, my brethren, though a man say he hath faith, and have not works? can faith save him? If a brother or sister be naked, and destitute of daily food, and one of you say unto them, Depart in peace, be ye warmed and filled; notwithstanding ye give them not those things which are needful to the body; what doth it profit? Even so faith, if it hath not works, is dead, being alone. Yea, a man may say, Thou hast faith, and I have works: shew me thy faith without thy works, and I will shew thee my faith by my works. Thou believest that there is one God; thou doest well: the devils also believe, and tremble. But wilt thou know, O vain man, that faith without works is dead? Was not Abraham our father justified by works, when he had offered Isaac his son upon the altar? Seest thou how faith wrought with his works, and by works was faith made perfect? And the scripture was fulfilled which saith, Abraham believed God, and it was imputed unto him for righteousness: and he was called the Friend of God. Ye see then how that by works a man is justified, and not by faith only. Likewise also was not Rahab the harlot justified by works, when she had received the messengers, and had sent them out another way? For as the body without the spirit is dead, so faith without works is dead also."

In this passage, James gives several examples to illustrate the connection between faith and works. He speaks of a Christian who sends away a fellow believer, hungry and naked, with mere empty words of comfort, but without food or clothing. He speaks of the devils—or demons—who believe in the existence of the one true God, but find no comfort, but only fear, in their belief. He speaks of Abraham offering his son Isaac in sacrifice to God. And he speaks of the harlot Rahab, in Jericho, receiving and protecting Joshua's messengers. However, it is in the last verse, verse 26, that James sums up his teaching about the connection between faith and works by the example of the relationship between the body and the spirit. He says: "For as the body without the spirit is dead, so faith without works is dead also."

It is this reference to "the spirit," in connection with faith, that provides the key to the proper understanding of the operation of faith in the life of the believer.

In an earlier study on faith we have already referred to the words of Paul in Second Corinthians, chapter 4, verse 13: "We having the same **spirit of faith**, according as it is written, I believed, and therefore have I spoken; we also believe, and therefore speak."

Here Paul states that true, scriptural faith is something spiritual—it is "the spirit of faith." Through this we are able to understand James' example of the body and the spirit. In the natural order, so long as a man is alive, his spirit dwells within his body. The spirit is itself invisible, but from within it directs and controls all that the man does with his body. Every action of the man's body is an expression of his spirit within him. Thus, the actual existence and character of the spirit within the man, though invisible, are clearly revealed through the behaviour and the actions of the man's body. When the spirit finally leaves the man's body, then the body ceases from all its actions and becomes lifeless. The lifeless inactivity of the body indicates that the spirit no longer dwells within.

So it is with the "spirit of faith" within the true Christian. This spirit of faith is alive and active. It brings down the very life of God Himself, in Christ, to dwell within the believer's heart. This life of God, within the believer, takes control of the whole nature of the believer—his desires, his thoughts, his words, his actions. The believer begins to think, to speak, and to act in an entirely new way—a way that is totally different from what he would have done previously. He says and does things which he neither could nor would have done before the life of God came in, through faith, to take control of him. Thus, his new way of living—his new "works," as James calls it—is the evidence and the expression of the faith within his heart. But if none of the outward actions are manifested in the man's life—none of the works that correspond to the faith which he professes—then this proves that there is no real living faith within him. Without this real living faith, expressed in corresponding actions, his profession of Christianity is no better than a dead body, after the spirit has left it.

We may briefly consider, in order, each of the four examples which James gives, and see how each illustrates this principle:

First, James speaks of the Christian who sees a fellow Christian naked and hungry, and says to him, "Depart in peace, be warmed and filled," but nevertheless does not offer him either food or clothing. Obviously, this man's words were not sincere. If he had really desired to see the other person warmed and fed, he would have given him food and clothing. The fact that he did not do it indicates that he did not really care. His words were a mere empty profession, without any inward reality. So it is when a Christian professes faith, but does not act according to the faith which he professes. Such faith is insincere, worthless, dead.

Secondly, James speaks of the demons who believe in the one true God, but temble. These demons have no doubt whatever about the existence of God, but they know also that they are the unrepentant enemies of God, under his sentence of wrath and judgment. Therefore, their faith brings them no comfort, but only fear. This shows that true, scriptural faith is always expressed in submission and obedience to God. Faith that continues stubborn and disobedient is dead faith, that cannot save from God's wrath and judgment.

Thirdly, James gives us the same example of faith as that given by Paul in Romans chapter 4—the example of Abraham. In Genesis chapter 15, verse 6, we read that Abraham "believed God, and it was counted to him for righteousness." Living faith in God's Word came into Abraham's heart at this time. Thereafter, this faith was expressed outwardly in a continual walk of submission and obedience to God. Each act of obedience that Abraham performed developed and strengthened his faith, and made him ready for the next act.

The final test of Abraham's faith came in Genesis chapter 22, when God asked him to offer up his son Isaac in sacrifice. Concerning this we read in Hebrews chapter 11, verses 17 and 19: "**By faith** Abraham, when he was tried, offered up Isaac . . . accounting that God was able to raise him up, even from the dead . . ." By this time, through continual exercise in obedience, Abraham's faith had been developed and strengthened even to the place where he really believed that God could raise up and restore his son to him from the dead. This faith in Abraham's heart found its outward expression in his perfect willingness to offer up Isaac, and it was only the direct intervention of God that kept him from actually slaying his son. Concerning this, James says: "Faith wrought with his works, and by works was faith made perfect." Thus we may sum up Abraham's experience as follows: His walk with God began with faith in his heart in God's Word. This faith expressed itself outwardly in a life of submission and obedience. Each act of obedience strengthened and developed his faith, and made him ready for the next test. Finally, this interworking of faith and works in his life brought him to the climax of his faith—to the point where he was willing even to offer up Isaac.

The fourth example which James gives of the relation between faith and works is that of Rahab. The story of Rahab is related in chapter 2 and chapter 6 of the book of Joshua. Rahab was a sinful, Canaanite woman, living in the city of Jericho, which was under the sentence of God's wrath and judgment. Having heard of the miraculous way in which God had led Israel out of Egypt, Rahab had come to believe that the God of Israel was the true God, and that he would give Canaan and its inhabitants into the hand of His people Israel. However, Rahab also believed that the God of Israel was merciful enough and powerful enough to save her and her family alive. This was the faith that Rahab had in her heart.

This faith in Rahab's heart found expression in two things that she then did. First, when Joshua sent two men ahead of his army into Jericho, Rahab received these two men into her home, hid them, and enabled them to escape again. In doing this, Rahab risked her own life. Later, in order to claim God's protection upon her home and family, she hung a line of scarlet from her window, to distinguish her house from all the others. This was the same window that Rahab had previously helped the two men to escape through. As a result of these two acts of Rahab, her house and family were saved from the destruction that later came upon all the rest of Jericho. Had Rahab merely believed secretly in her heart in the God of Israel, but been unwilling to perform these two acts of faith, her faith would have been merely a dead faith, and it would have had no power to save her from the judgment that came upon Jericho.

The lesson for us as Christians is that, if we profess faith in Christ, we must be willing to identify ourselves actively with Christ's cause, and Christ's messengers, even though it may mean real personal sacrifice, perhaps the risking or laying down of our very lives. Secondly, we must be willing to make a definite, open confession of our faith, that marks us out from all the unbelievers round about us. The scarlet line speaks particularly of openly confessing our faith in the blood of Christ for the remission and cleansing of our sin.

* * *

For a final summary of the relation between faith and works we may turn once again to the writings of Paul.

In Philippians, chapter 2, verses 12 and 13, Paul says: "Work out your own salvation with fear and trembling. For it is God which worketh in you both to will and to do of his good pleasure." Here the relationship is plain. First, God works in us both to will and to do. Then we work out, in our actions, that which God has first worked in us.

The important thing to realize is that faith comes first, then works. We receive salvation from God by faith alone, without works. Once having received salvation in this way, we then work it out actively in our lives by our works—by the things that we do. If we do not actively work out our salvation this way, after believing, this shows that the faith which we have professed is merely dead faith, and that we have no real experience of salvation.

We do not receive salvation by works. But our works are the test of whether our faith is real and the means by which our faith is developed. Only real, living faith can make a real, living Christian.

VI
Law And Grace

The Law Of Moses One Single Complete System—Given Only To Israel—Does Not Apply To Christians

Welcome to the Study Hour.

Our textbook—the Bible.

The study which we shall now bring you today is No. 14 in our present series, entitled "Foundations."

We are at present engaged in a systematic examination of the six great foundation doctrines of the Christian faith, as stated in Hebrews, chapter 6, verses 1 and 2. Our last four studies in this series have all centred around the second of these six great foundation doctrines—that which is called in Hebrews, chapter 6, verse 1, "faith toward God"—or, more simply, "faith."

After first discussing the nature of faith, as defined in the scriptures, we then went on to examine, in our previous study, the relationship between faith and works—between what we believe, and what we do. In our study today we shall proceed further into this same subject—the relationship between faith and works.

In our previous study we came to the following conclusion: According to the New Testament, salvation is received through faith alone—faith in Christ's finished work of atonement—without human works of any kind. But thereafter the faith which brings salvation always issues in appropriate works—actions which correspond with the faith that has been professed. It is by these appropriate works— these corresponding actions—that faith is naturally and inevitably expressed and developed. A faith that does not produce these appropriate works is a mere empty profession—a dead faith—incapable of bringing a real experience of salvation.

* * *

This conclusion concerning the relationship between faith and works naturally leads us to ask a further question: What are the works by which genuine saving faith is expressed? What are the works which we should expect to see in the life of every person who exercises genuine scriptural faith for salvation?

This is obviously a question of great practical importance for all sincere Christians, but it is one which preachers seldom seem to deal with in a plain and practical way. We shall therefore devote our study today to seeking, from the pages of the New Testament, the answer to this question: What are the works which we should look for in the life of every person who professes faith in Christ for salvation?

The first thing which needs to be stated with clarity and with emphasis is this: Saving faith is **not** expressed by keeping the law, either wholly or in part. According to the New Testament, the believer who has been justified by faith in Christ is not thereafter required to observe any part of the law of Moses.

This is a subject on which there is a great deal of confused thinking and speaking among Christians. In order to clear up the confusion, there are first of all certain basic facts about the law which we must recognize.

The first great fact, very plainly stated in scripture, is that the law was given complete, once for all, by Moses. This is made plain in John's Gospel, chapter 1, verse 17: "For **the law** was given by Moses, but grace and truth came by Jesus Christ." Notice that phrase, "the law was given by Moses." Not "some laws," or "part of the law," but "the law"—the whole law—complete and entire in one system—was given at one period in history and through the human instrumentality of one man only—and that man was Moses. Everywhere in scripture, unless some special qualifying phrase is added to modify or change the meaning, the phrase, "the law", denotes always and only the complete system of law given by God through Moses.

Confirmation of this is found in Romans chapter 5, verses 13 and 14: "For **until the law** sin was in the world: but sin is not imputed when there is no law. Nevertheless, death reigned **from Adam to Moses**, even over them that had not sinned after the similitude of Adam's transgression . . . " Notice the two phrases indicating a definite period of time: "until the law," and "from Adam to Moses." When God created Adam and placed him in the garden, He gave him not a complete system of law, but a single negative commandment, "Thou shalt not eat of the fruit of the tree that is in the midst of the garden." Adam transgressed against this commandment, and sin entered into the human race, and passed upon Adam and upon all his descendants from that time onward. The evidence that sin passed upon all men from the time of Adam onward is found in the fact that all men became liable to death, which is the outcome of sin. However, from the time that Adam transgressed against that first, single God-given commandment until the time of Moses, there was no God-given, God-enforced system of law revealed and applied to the human race. This explains how the two phrases "until the law" and "from Adam to Moses" denote the same period of human history—the period from Adam's transgression of the single commandment in the garden down to the time when the complete system of divine law was given by God through Moses. During this period the human race was without any system of God-given, God-enforced law. This is in full accord with the statement already quoted from John's Gospel, chapter 1, verse 17: "The law was given by Moses."

This law, so given, was a single, complete system of commandments, statutes, ordinances and judgments. All these are contained, in their entirety, within the compass of four books of the Bible. These are the books of Exodus, Leviticus, Numbers and Deuteronomy. Before the time of Moses and of the events recorded in these books, there was no divine system of law given to the human race. Furthermore, after the close of this period and of these books, nothing further was ever added to this system of law. That the law was thus given once for all, complete, is made plain by the words of Moses in Deuteronomy chapter 4, verses 1 and 2: "Now therefore hearken, O Israel, unto the statutes and unto the judgments, which I teach you, for to do them, that ye may live, and go in and possess the land which the Lord God of your fathers giveth you. Ye shall not add unto the word which I command you, neither shall ye diminish ought from it, that ye may keep the commandments of the Lord your God which I command you." These words show that the system of law given by God to Israel through Moses was complete and final. Thereafter nothing more was ever to be added to it, and nothing was ever to be diminished—or taken away—from it.

This leads us naturally to the next great fact which must be clearly established in relation to the keeping of the law: every person who comes under the law is thereby obliged to observe the **whole** system of law in its entirety and **at all times**. There is no question of observing certain parts of the law and omitting certain other parts. Nor is there any question of keeping the law at certain times and failing to keep it at other times. Any person who comes under the law is necessarily obliged to keep **the whole law at all times**.

This is very plainly stated in the Epistle of James, chapter 2, verses 10 and 11: "For whosoever shall keep the whole law, and yet offend in one point, he is guilty of all. For he that said, Do not commit adultery, said also, Do not kill. Now if thou commit no adultery, yet if thou kill, thou art become a transgressor of the law." This is very plain and very logical. A person cannot say: "I consider certain points of the law to be important, so I will observe these; but I consider certain other points of the law to be unimportant, so I will not observe those." Any person who seeks to observe any points of the law must observe them all. Conversely, a person who breaks only one point of the law has thereby broken the whole law. The law is a single, complete system, which cannot be divided up into some points which are applied and others which are not applied. The whole law must be accepted and applied, complete and entire, as a single system, or else it is of no benefit or validity whatever.

This is stated no less plainly by the apostle Paul in Galatians chapter 3, verse 10: "For as many as are of the works of the law are under the curse: for it is written, Cursed is everyone that **continueth not** in **all** things which are written in the book of the law to do them." Notice that phrase: "**continueth** . . . in **all** things." This indicates that a person who is under the law must observe the **whole** law at **all** times. A person who at any time breaks any point of the law has transgressed against the whole law, and has thus come under the divine curse pronounced upon all transgressors of the law.

Following on from this, we come to the third important fact which must be recognized in connection with the law, and this is a matter of actual historical fact: The system of law given by Moses was ordained by God solely for one small section of the human race, and that was the people of Israel, after their deliverance from the bondage of Egypt. Nowhere in the Bible is there any suggestion that God ever intended that the Gentiles, either nationally or individually, should observe the law of Moses, either wholly or in part. The only exception to this is found in the case of a few individual Gentiles who voluntarily decided to associate themselves with Israel and thereby to place themselves under all the legal and religious obligations which God had imposed upon Israel. Such Gentile converts to Judaism are in the New Testament called "proselytes." Apart from these, the obligations of the law have never been imposed by God upon any Gentile.

Thus we may briefly sum up the three important facts which it is necessary for us to recognize before we study in detail the relationship of the Christian believer to the law: First, the law was given once for all, as a single, complete system, by Moses; thereafter, nothing could ever be added to it, or taken from it. Second, the law must always be observed in its entirety as a single, complete system; to break any one point of the law is to break the whole law. Third, as a matter of human history, this system of law was never ordained by God for Gentiles, but only for Israel.

* * *

Having established these three facts as a basis, we may now go on to examine in detail what the New Testament teaches about the relation between the Christian believer and the law. This question is referred to in many different passages of the New Testament, and in every passage the same clear, definite truth is taught. The Christian believer is not required to observe any part of the law.

Let us look at a number of passages in the New Testament which make this plain.

First of all, there is Romans chapter 6, verse 14, which is addressed directly to Christian believers: "For sin shall not have dominion over you: for ye are **not under the law, but under grace.**" This verse reveals two important truths. First, Christian believers are not under the law, but under grace. These are two alternatives which mutually exclude each other: a person who is under the law is not under grace; a person who is under grace is not under the law. No person can be under both the law and grace at the same time. Secondly, the very reason why sin shall not have dominion over Christian believers is because they are not under the law. So long as a person is under the law he is also under the dominion of sin. To escape from the dominion of sin a person must come out from under the law.

This is confirmed by what Paul says in First Corinthians chapter 15, verse 56: "The sting of death is sin; and **the strength of sin is the law.**" The law actually strengthens the dominion of sin over those who are under the law. The harder they strive to keep the law, the more conscious they become of the power of sin within themselves, exercising dominion over them, even against their own will, and frustrating every attempt to live by the law. The only excape from this dominion of sin is to come out from under the law and to come under grace.

The same truth is expressed again by Paul in Romans chapter 7, verses 5 and 6: "For when we were in the flesh, the motions—or passions—of sins, which were by the law, did work in our members to bring forth fruit unto death. **But now we are delivered from the law,** that being dead wherein we were held; that we should serve in newness of spirit, and not in the oldness of the letter." Here Paul says that those who are under the law are subject to the motions, or passions, of sin in their fleshly nature, which cause them to bring forth fruit unto death; but that, as Christian believers, "we are **delivered from the law,**" that we should serve God, not according to the letter of the law, but in the newness of spiritual life which we receive

page sixty-seven

through faith.

Again, in Romans chapter 10, verse 4, Paul says: "For Christ is **the end of the law** for righteousness **to every one that believeth.**" As soon as a person puts his faith in Christ for salvation and righteousness, that is the end of the law, for that person, as a means of righteousness. Paul here is very careful and precise in what he says. He does not say that there is an end of the law as a part of God's Word. On the contrary, God's Word "endureth forever." There is an end of the law, for the believer, as a means of righteousness. The believer's righteousness is no longer derived from the keeping of the law, either wholly or in part, but solely from faith in Christ.

The truth that the law as a means of righteousness came to an end with the atoning death of Christ upon the cross is stated again by Paul in Colossians chapter 2, verses 13 and 14: "And you, being dead in your sins, and the uncircumcision of your flesh, hath he (God) quickened together with him (Christ), having forgiven you all trespasses; blotting out the **handwriting of ordinances** that was against us, which was contrary to us, **and took it out of the way,** nailing it to his cross . . . " Here Paul states that, through the death of Christ, God "blotted out the **handwriting of ordinances** that was against us," and "took it out of the way." Paul here does not speak about the blotting out of sins, but about the blotting out of ordinances. These ordinances are the ordinances of the law, which stood between God and those who had transgressed them, and therefore had to be taken out of the way before God could bestow mercy and forgiveness upon them. The word "ordinances" here denotes the whole system of law which God had ordained through Moses, including that particular section of the law which we usually call "the ten commandments." In fact, the very word "handwriting," used here in connection with the "ordinances," refers to the fact that those ten commandments were actually written by the finger of God Himself, as is stated in Exodus chapter 32, verse 16, and chapter 34, verse 1.

This reference to the ten commandments is confirmed by what Paul says two verses on in the same second chapter of Colossians; that is, in Colossians chapter 2, verse 16: "Let no man **therefore** judge you in meat, or in drink, or in respect of an holyday, or of the new moon, or of **the sabbath days.**" The word "therefore" at the opening of this verse indicates a direct connection with that which had been stated two verses previously; that is, the blotting out of the ordinances of the law through the death of Christ. Again, the mention of "the sabbath days" at the end of the verse indicates that the religious observance of the sabbath day was included among those ordinances which had been blotted out. Yet the commandment to observe the sabbath day is the fourth of the ten commandments. This indicates that the ten commandments are included among the totality of the ordinances of the law that have been blotted out and taken out of the way through the death of Christ.

This confirms that which we have already established, that the law, including the ten commandments, is a single, complete system, which stands or falls as one whole. It was introduced as a single system, complete, by Moses; and it was done away as a single system, complete, by Christ.

Yet further confirmation is found in the words of Paul in Ephesians chapter 2, verses 14 and 15:

"For he (Christ) is our peace, who hath made both one, and hath broken down the middle wall of partition between us; **Having abolished** in his flesh the enmity, even **the law of commandments** contained in ordinances; for to make in himself of twain one new man, so making peace."

Paul here tells us that Christ, through His atoning death on the cross, has "abolished—that is, made of no effect—**the law of commandments**"; and that He has thereby taken away the great dividing line of the law of Moses, which separated Jews from Gentiles, making it possible for Jews and Gentiles alike, through faith in Christ, to be reconciled both with God and with each other. The phrase, "the law of commandments," indicates as plainly as possible that the entire law of Moses, **including the ten commandments,** was made of no further effect, as a means of righteousness, by the death of Christ upon the cross.

page sixty-nine

In First Timothy chapter 1, verses 8, 9 and 10, Paul again discusses the relationship of the Christian believer to the law, and reaches the same conclusion, for he says: "But we know that the law is good, if a man use it lawfully; knowing this, that the law is not made for a righteous man, but for the lawless and disobedient, for the ungodly and for sinners, for unholy and profane, for murderers of fathers and murderers of mothers, for manslayers, for whoremongers, for them that defile themselves with mankind, for menstealers, for liars, for perjured persons, and if there be any other thing that is contrary to sound doctrine." Here Paul defines two classes of persons: on the one hand, there is a righteous man; on the other hand, there are those guilty of the various sins enumerated in Paul's list. A person guilty of these sins is not a true believing Christian; such a person has not been saved from sin by faith in Christ. On the other hand, a person who trusts Christ for salvation is no longer guilty of such sins; he has been justified, he has been made righteous—not with his own righteousness, but with the righteousness of God "which is by faith of Jesus Christ unto all and upon all them that believe." Paul says clearly that the law is not made for a righteous man such as this; he is no longer under the dominion of the law.

Again, in Romans chapter 8, verse 14, Paul says: "For as many as are led by the Spirit of God, they are the sons of God." That is, God's true, believing children in Christ are those who are led by God's Spirit—that is what marks them out as children of God. Concerning such people as this, Paul says in Galatians chapter 5, verse 18: "But if ye be led of the Spirit, ye are not under the law." Thus, the very thing which marks out the true, believing children of God—being led of God's Spirit—also means that such people are not under the law. We may put it briefly and personally in this way: If you are a true child of God by faith in Christ, the evidence is that you are led by the Spirit of God. But if you are led by the Spirit of God, then you are not under the law. Therefore, you cannot be a child of God and under the law at the same time. More simply still, God's children are not under the law.

We may illustrate this contrast between the law and

the Spirit by the example of trying to find the way to a certain place by two different means: one means is to use a map; the other means is to follow a personal guide. The law corresponds to the map; the Holy Spirit corresponds to the guide. Under the law, a person is given a completely accurate and detailed map, and he is told that if he follows every detail of the map faultlessly, it will direct him on the way from earth to heaven. However, no human being has ever succeeded in following the map faultlessly. That is, no human being has ever made the journey from earth to heaven by the faultless observation of the law. Under grace, a person commits himself to Christ as Saviour, and thereafter Christ sends the Holy Spirit to that person to be his personal Guide. The Holy Spirit, having come from heaven, already knows the way to heaven, and has no need of the help of the map. That is, the believer in Christ who is led by the Holy Spirit needs only to follow this personal guide to reach heaven, and does not need the direction of the map, which is the law. Therefore, the New Testament teaches, perfectly logically, that those who are under grace are led by God's Spirit and do not need the help of the law.

We conclude, therefore, that God has never actually expected men to achieve true righteousness by the observance of the law, either wholly or in part.

This conclusion naturally raises a very interesting question: If God never expected men to achieve righteousness by the observance of the law, for what purpose was the law ever given to men?

In our next study in this series we shall take up this question, and we shall suggest a number of interesting answers to it, based on the revelation of the New Testament.

VII
The Purpose Of The Law

To Reveal Sin—To Prove Man's Inability To Save Himself—To Foreshow Christ—To Preserve Israel—Perfectly Fulfilled By Christ

Welcome to the Study Hour.

Our textbook—the Bible.

The study which we shall now bring you today is No. 15 in our present series, entitled "Foundations."

We are at present engaged in a systematic examination of the six great foundation doctrines of the Christian faith, as stated in Hebrews chapter 6, verses 1 and 2. Our recent studies have all centred around the second of these great foundation doctrines, that which is called in Hebrews chapter 6, verse 1, "faith toward God," or, more simply, "faith." In particular, in our last two studies we have been examining the relationship between faith and works—between what we believe and what we do. In this connection, we have so far reached the following three main conclusions:

First, according to the New Testament, salvation is received through faith alone—faith in Christ's finished work of atonement—without human works of any kind.

Second, the faith which brings salvation always issues in appropriate works—actions which correspond with the faith that has been professed. It is by these appropriate works—these corresponding actions—that faith is naturally and inevitably expressed and developed. A faith that does not produce these appropriate works is a mere empty profession—a dead faith—incapable of bringing a real experience of salvation.

Third, the works by which saving faith is expressed are never "the works of the law." According to the New Testament, the believer who has been justified by faith in Christ is not thereafter required to observe any part of the law of Moses. In fact, God never actually expected men to achieve true righteousness by the observance of the law, either wholly or in part.

This third conclusion which we have just stated naturally raises a very interesting question: If God never expected men to achieve righteousness by the observance of the law, for what purpose was the law ever given to men?

We shall now proceed to put forward a number of interesting answers to this question, based on the revelation of the New Testament.

* * *

For what purposes was the law ever given to men?

The first main purpose, as revealed in the New Testament, is this: The law was given to show men their sinful condition.

This is clearly stated by the apostle Paul in Romans chapter 3, verses 19 and 20: "Now we know that what things soever the law saith, it saith to them who are under the law: that every mouth may be stopped, and **all the world may become guilty** before God. Therefore, by the deeds of the law there shall no flesh be justified in his sight: **for by the law is the knowledge of sin.**"

Notice first of all the very definite statement: "By the deeds of the law there shall no flesh be justified in God's sight." In other words, no human being will ever achieve righteousness in God's sight by the observance of the law.

Side by side with this, Paul states twice, in two different phrases, the primary purpose for which the law was given. He says, first, "that all the world may become guilty before God." An alternative translation is, "that all the world may become subject to the judgment of God." Secondly, he says, "by the law is the knowledge of sin."

We see, therefore, that the law was not given to make men righteous, but—on the contrary—to make men conscious that they were sinners, and, as such, subject to the judgment of God upon their sin.

Paul states the same truth again in Romans chapter 7, verse 7, and also verses 12 and 13.

In verse 7 he says: "What shall we say then? Is the

law sin? God forbid. Nay, **I had not known sin, but by the law:** for I had not known lust, except the law had said, Thou shalt not covet."

Again in verses 12 and 13 he says: "Wherefore the law is holy, and the commandment holy, and just, and good. Was then that which is good made death unto me? God forbid. But **sin, that it might appear sin,** working death in me by that which is good; that **sin by the commandment might become exceeding sinful.**"

Notice three phrases which Paul uses in these verses, all bringing out the same truth: "I had not known sin, but by the law"; "sin, that it might appear sin"; "that sin by the commandment might become exceeding sinful." In other words, the purpose of the law was to bring sin right out into the open—to show sin in its true colours, as the subtle, destructive, deadly thing that it really is. Thereafter men were left without any excuse for being deceived as to the extreme sinfulness of their condition.

In the practice of medicine, when treating diseases of the human body, there is a certain order which is always followed: first the diagnosis; then the remedy. First of all, the doctor examines the sick man, and tries to ascertain the nature and cause of his disease; only after he has done that, does he attempt to prescribe a remedy. Very logically, God follows the same order in dealing with man's spiritual need. Before prescribing the cure, God first diagnoses the condition. The basic cause of all human need and suffering lies in one condition common to all members of the human race, and that condition is "sin." No satisfactory remedy for human needs can be offered, until this condition has first been diagnosed. The Bible is the only book in the world which clearly and correctly diagnoses the cause of all humanity's need and suffering. For this reason alone— apart from all else that it has to offer—the Bible is both invaluable and irreplaceable.

* * *

The second main purpose for which the law was given was to show men that, as sinners, they are unable to make themselves righteous by their own efforts. There is a natural tendency in every human being to desire to be independent of God's grace and mercy. This desire to be independent of God is in itself both a result and an evidence of man's sinful condition, although most men do not recognize it as such. Thus, whenever a man becomes convicted of his sinful condition, his first reaction is to seek some means by which he can cure himself of this condition and make himself righteous by his own efforts, without having to depend on the grace and mercy of God. For this reason, throughout all ages religious laws and observances have always made a strong appeal to the human race, regardless of differences of nationality or background. In practising such laws and observances men have sought to silence the inward voice of their own conscience and to make themselves righteous by their own efforts.

This was precisely the reaction of many religious Israelites to the law of Moses. Paul describes this attempt of Israel to establish their own righteousness in Romans chapter 10, verse 3: "For they being ignorant of God's righteousness, and going about to establish their own righteousness, have not submitted themselves unto the righteousness of God." Notice that, as a result of Israel's attempting to establish their own righteousness, they failed to submit themselves to God and to God's way of righteousness. Thus, the basic cause of their error was spiritual pride—a refusal to submit themselves to God—a desire to be independent of God's grace and mercy.

However, whenever men are really willing to face facts and to be honest with themselves, they are always obliged to admit that they can never succeed in making themselves righteous by the observing of religious or moral law. In Romans chapter 7, verses 18 through 23, Paul describes this in the first person as being an experience through which he himself had at one time passed in his efforts to make himself righteous by the observance of the law. Here is what he says: "For I know that in me (that is, in my flesh,) dwelleth no good thing: for to will is present with me; but how to perform that which is good I find not. For the good that I would I do not: but the evil which I would not, that I do. Now if I do that I would not, it is no more I that do it, but sin that dwelleth in me. I find then a law, that, when I would do good, evil is present with me. For I delight in the law of God after the inward man: But I see another law in my members, warring against the law of my mind, and bringing me into captivity to the law of sin which is in my members."

Here Paul speaks as one who sincerely acknowledges with his mind the righteousness and the desirability of the way of life which the law enjoins. The more he struggles to do what the law commands, the more he becomes conscious of another law, another power, within his own fleshly nature, continually warring against the law which his mind acknowledges, and frustrating his strongest and sincerest efforts to make himself righteous by observing the law. The central point of this inward conflict is expressed in verse 21: "I find them a law, that, when I would do good, evil is present with me." This is an apparent paradox, yet it is confirmed by all human experience. A man never knows how bad he is, until he really tries to be good. Thereafter, every attempt to be good only brings out more clearly the hopeless, incurable sinfulness of his own fleshly nature, in face of which all his efforts and good intentions are entirely in vain.

We find, then, that the second main purpose for which the law was given was to shown men that not merely are they sinful, but furthermore they are wholly unable to save themselves from sin and make themselves righteous by their own efforts.

* * *

The third main purpose for which the law was given was to foretell and to foreshadow the Saviour who was to come, and through whom alone it would be possible for man to receive true salvation and righteousness. This was done through the law in two main ways: the Saviour was **foretold** through direct prophecy and He was **foreshadowed** through the types and ceremonies of the ordinances of the law.

An example of direct prophecy, within the framework of the law, is found in Deuteronomy chapter 18, verses 18 and 19, where the Lord says to Israel through Moses: "I will raise them up a Prophet from among their brethren, like unto thee, and will put my words in his mouth; and he shall speak unto them all that I shall command him. And it shall come to pass, that whosoever will not hearken unto my words which he shall speak in my name, I will require it of him." In Acts chapter 3, verses 22 through 26, these words of Moses are quoted by the apostle Peter, and are directly applied by him to the Lord Jesus Christ. Thus, the Prophet foretold by Moses in the law is fulfilled in the person of Christ in the New Testament.

In the sacrifices and ordinances of the law there are many types which prophetically foreshadow Jesus Christ as the Saviour who was to come. For example, in Exodus chapter 12, the ordinance of the Passover lamb prophetically foreshadows salvation through faith in the atoning blood of Jesus Christ, shed at the Passover season upon the cross at Calvary. Similarly, the various sacrifices connected with expiation of sin and approach to God, described in the first seven chapters of the book of Leviticus, all foreshadow various aspects of the sacrificial, atoning death of Jesus Christ upon the cross. For this reason, in John's Gospel chapter 1, verse 29, we read how John the Baptist introduced Christ to Israel with these words: "Behold the Lamb of God, which taketh away the sin of the world." By the comparison of Christ to a sacrificial lamb, the people of Israel were directed to see in Christ the One who had been foreshadowed by all the sacrificial ordinances of the law.

This purpose of the law is summed up in the words of Paul in Galatians chapter 3, verses 22, 23 and 24: "But the scripture hath concluded all under sin, that the promise by faith of Jesus Christ might be given to them that believe. But before faith came, we were kept under the law, shut up unto the faith which should afterwards be revealed. Wherefore **the law was our schoolmaster to bring us unto Christ,** that we might be justified by faith."

The Greek word here translated "schoolmaster" denotes actually a senior slave in the household of a wealthy man, whose special responsibility it was to give the first elementary stages of teaching to the wealthy man's children, and thereafter to escort them each day to the school, where they could receive further, more advanced instruction. In a corresponding way, the law gave Israel their first elementary instruction in God's basic requirements concerning righteousness, and thereafter it was a means to direct them to put their faith in Jesus Christ and to learn from Christ the lesson of the true righteousness which is by faith, without the works of the law. Just as this slave's educational task was complete as soon as he had delivered his master's children into the care of the fully-trained teacher in the school, so the law's task was complete once it had brought Israel to their Messiah, Jesus Christ, and had caused them to see their need of salvation through faith in Him.

* * *

In the words of Paul already quoted from Galatians chapter 3, verse 23, there is a phrase which reveals one further important function of the law, in connection with Israel. Speaking as an Israelite, Paul says: "We were **kept under the law, shut up** unto the faith which should afterwards be revealed." The law kept Israel as a special nation, set apart from all others, separated out by its distinctive rites and ordinances, shut up unto the special purposes for which God had called them. In Numbers chapter 23, verse 9, the prophet Balaam, in his God-given vision of Israel's destiny, sets forth God's plan for them: "Lo, the people (Israel) shall dwell alone, and shall not be reckoned among the nations." God's perfect will for Israel was that thy should "dwell alone," as a unique and separate nation, in their own land. But even when Israel's disobedience frustrated this first purpose of God for them and caused them to be scattered as exiles and wanderers among all nations of the world, God still ordained that "they should not be reckoned among the nations." In the past nineteen centuries of Jewish dispersion among the Gentile nations, this decree of God concerning them has always been most wonderfully fulfilled. In all the lands and nations whither they have come, the Jews have always remained a distinct and separate element which has never been assimilated or lost its special identity. The main instrument used in the providence of God for thus keeping Israel a separate nation has been their continued adherence to the law of Moses.

In conclusion, we may sum up the four main purposes for which the law of Moses was given: **First,** the law was given to show men their sinful condition. **Second,** the law also showed men that, as sinners, they were unable to make themselves righteous by their own efforts. **Third,** the law served to foretell by prophecy, and to foreshadow by types, the Saviour who was to come, and through whom alone it would be possible for man to receive true salvation and righteousness. **Fourth,** the law has served to keep Israel a separate nation throughout the many centuries of their dispersion, so that even now they are still shut up unto the special purposes which God is working out for them.

* * *

Our examination of the relationship between the law and the gospel could not be complete without taking into account the words in which Christ Himself sums up His attitude and His relationship to the law. These words are found in Matthew's Gospel chapter 5, verses 17 and 18: "Think not that I am come to destroy the law, or the prophets: I am not come to destroy, but to fulfil. For verily I say unto you, Till heaven and earth pass, one jot or one tittle shall in no wise pass from the law, till all be fulfilled."

In what sense did Christ fulfil the law?

First of all, He personally fulfilled it by His own spotless righteousness and by the faultless, consistent observance of every ordinance. In Galatians chapter 4, verses 4 and 5, we read: "God sent forth his Son, made of a woman, **made under the law,** to redeem them that were under the law, that we might receive the adoption of sons." Notice the words: "made of a woman, made under the law." By His birth as a man, Jesus Christ was a Jew, subject to all the ordinances and obligations of the law. These He perfectly fulfilled throughout the entire course of His life on earth, without ever deviating one hair's breadth from all that was required of every Jew under the law. In this sense, Jesus Christ alone, of all those who ever came under the law, perfectly fulfilled it.

Secondly, Jesus Christ fulfilled the law in another sense by His atoning death on the cross. The apostle Peter speaks of this in his First Epistle, chapter 2, verses 22 and 24. Referring to Christ, Peter says here: "Who did no sin, neither was guile found in his mouth . . . Who his own self bare our sins in his own body on the tree, that we, being dead to sins, should live unto righteousness . . ." Himself without sin, Christ took upon Himself the sins of all those who had been under the law, and then paid in full on behalf of them all the law's final penalty, which is death. With the full penalty thus paid by Christ, it became possible for God, without compromising His divine justice, to offer full and free pardon to all who by faith accept Christ's atoning death on their behalf. Thus Christ fulfilled the law first by His life of perfect righteousness, and second by His atoning death, through which He satisfied the law's just demand upon all those who had not perfectly observed it.

Thirdly, Christ fulfilled the law by combining in Himself every feature prophetically set forth, in the law, of the Saviour and Messiah whom God had promised to send. Already, at the beginning of Christ's earthly ministry, in John's Gospel chapter 1, verse 45, we read how Philip said to Nathanael: 'We have found him, of whom **Moses in the law**, and the prophets, did write, Jesus of Nazareth, the son of Joseph." Again, after Christ's death and resurrection, in Luke's Gospel chapter 24, verse 44, we read how He Himself said unto them: "These are the words which I spake unto you, while I was yet with you, that all things must be fulfilled, which were written **in the law of Moses,** and in the prophets, and in the psalms, concerning me."

We find, then, that Christ fulfilled the law in three ways: first, by His perfect life; second, by His redeeming death and resurrection; third, by fulfilling all that the law foretold and foreshadowed concerning the Saviour and Messiah who was to come.

We thus find ourselves in perfect agreement with the words of Paul in Romans chapter 3, verse 31: "Do we then make void the law through faith? God forbid: yea, we establish the law." The believer who accepts the atoning death of Jesus Christ as the fulfilment of the law on his behalf is thereby enabled to accept, without compromise or qualification, every jot and tittle of the law as being completely and unchangeably true. Faith in Christ for salvation does not set aside the revelation of the law; on the contrary, it fulfils it.

Thus, we are brought back once again to the words of Paul in Romans chapter 10, verse 4: "For Christ is **the end of the law for righteousness** to every one that believeth." As a means whereby men may attain to righteousness, Christ did away with the law by paying once and for all the law's final penalty of death, on behalf of all those who were under the law. But in every other respect the law still stands, complete and entire, as a part of God's Word, which "endureth forever." Its history, its prophecy, and its general revelation of the mind and counsel of God—all these remain eternally and unchangeably true.

VIII
The True Righteousness

The Two Great Commandments—Love The Fulfilling Of The Law—The New Testament Pattern Of Obedience

Welcome to the Study Hour.

Our textbook—the Bible.

Once again today we present to you the Bible's own challenge: "Study for yourself!" Don't discuss a book that you have never studied. Don't be content with second-hand opinions, or traditions. Study for yourself! Find out first hand what the Bible really teaches. Then you will be in a position to form your own conclusions. You will be able to offer your own explanation as to why the Bible still remains today the most widely read and the most influential book in the entire history of the human race.

The study which we shall now bring you today is No. 16 in our present series, entitled "Foundations."

We are at present working our way systematically through the six great foundation doctrines of the Christian faith as stated in Hebrews chapter 6, verses 1 and 2. In our recent studies we have been examining, from different angles, the second of the six doctrines there listed—that which is called "faith toward God"—or, more simply, "faith."

In thus studying the nature of "faith," as defined in the Bible, we have been led to examine two subjects which are closely connected with "faith"; that is, the relationship between "faith" and "works," and, arising out of this, the relationship between "law" and "grace." Now, it must be frankly admitted that the majority of professing Christians today have given very little, if any, thought to either of these two subjects—the relationship between "faith" and "works," and the relationship between "law" and "grace." Yet an openminded examination of the New Testament would reveal that a great deal of close and careful attention is there given to these two subjects.

In this respect the condition of those Christians who have never given any thought to these subjects is somewhat similar to that of the man who went to the doctor complaining of a pain in his stomach. After some examination the doctor diagnosed the man's trouble as "appendicitis."

"Appendicitis!" said the man. "What's that?"

"Appendicitis," explained the doctor, "is a condition of irritation or inflamation of the appendix."

"Well," the man confessed, on hearing this explanation, "up till now I never even knew that I had an appendix to be inflamed!"

In a similar way, many professing Christians are conscious of some deep-seated trouble in their spiritual experience—trouble that finds expression in such symptoms as instability, inconsistency, lack of assurance, lack of peace. If such Christians were to be informed that the root cause of their trouble lay in the failure to understand such basic New Testament teachings as the relationship between "faith" and "works," or between "law" and "grace," these Christians would have to confess, just like the man with appendicitis, "Well, up till now, we never even knew that the New Testament had anything to say about such things as that!"

We may now briefly outline the conclusions which we have reached in studying these two related topics thus far. We have hitherto reached these main conclusions:

First, the whole New Testament teaches emphatically that salvation is received through faith alone—faith in Christ's finished work of atonement—without human works of any kind.

Second, the faith that brings salvation is always expressed thereafter in appropriate works—in corresponding actions.

Third, the works by which faith for salvation is expressed are never "the works of the law." That is, saving faith is never expressed by observing the law of Moses, either wholly or in part.

This third conclusion led us on to a further question:

If God never expected men to be made righteous by the keeping of the law, for what purpose was the law then given to men? In seeking the answer to this question, we concluded that the law was given by God for four main purposes: First, to show men the real nature and power of sin in their lives. Second, to show men that, as sinners, they were not able to make themselves righteous by their own efforts. Third, to foreshadow and foreshow, by type and prophecy, the Saviour who was to come, Jesus Christ, through faith in whom true salvation and righteousness would be made possible. Fourth, to keep Israel a separate nation, different from all other nations of the world, shut up unto the special purposes for which God had foreordained them and called them.

* * *

These conclusions concerning the nature and purpose of the law of Moses naturally lead us on to one further question: If saving faith is not expressed by the observance of the law, then what are the works by which saving faith is expressed? What are the appropriate actions which we should expect to see in the life of every person who has professed genuine saving faith in Christ?

The answer to this question, as well as the key to understanding the relationship between law and grace, is given by the apostle Paul in Romans chapter 8, verses 3 and 4: "For what the law could not do, in that it was weak through the flesh, God sending his own Son in the likeness of sinful flesh, and for sin, condemned sin in the flesh: that **the righteousness of the law** might be fulfilled in us, who walk not after the flesh, but after the Spirit."

The key phrase here is: "that the righteousness of the law might be fulfilled in us"—where "us" denotes Spirit-led Christians. It is not the law itself which is to be fulfilled in Christians, but the "righteousness of the law."

What is meant by this phrase, "the righteousness of the law"?

The answer to this question is given most clearly and precisely by Jesus Christ Himself in Matthew's Gospel, chapter 22, verses 35 through 40. These verses record a question asked by a Jewish lawyer concerning the law, and the answer which Jesus gave to that question.

"Then one of them, which was a lawyer, asked him a question, tempting him, and saying,

"Master, which is the great commandment in the law?

"Jesus said unto him, Thou shalt love the Lord thy God with all thy heart, and with all thy soul, and with all thy mind.

"This is the first and great commandment.

"And the second is like unto it, Thou shalt love thy neighbour as thyself.

"On these two commandments hang all the law and the prophets."

In these words Jesus very plainly defines "the righteousness of the law", to which Paul refers. The law of Moses was only given at a certain period in human history to a small section of the human race. But behind this complete system of law so given there stand the two great, eternal, unchanging laws of God for the whole human race: "Thou shalt love the Lord thy God," and "Thou shalt love thy neighbour as thyself." The system of law given through Moses was merely a detailed application and outworking of these two great basic commands—love for God, and love for our neighbour. On these two commandments depended the whole legal system of Moses and the entire ministry and message of all the Old Testament prophets. Here, then, is "the righteousness of the law," summed up in two all-inclusive commandments: "Love God," and "Love thy neighbour."

This same truth is taught again by Paul in his First Epistle to Timothy, chapter 1, verses 5, 6 and 7: "Now **the end of the commandment is charity** out of a pure heart, and of a good conscience, and of faith unfeigned: From which some having swerved have turned aside unto vain jangling; desiring to be teachers of the law; understanding neither what they say, nor whereof they affirm."

Notice that illuminating statement; "the end of the commandment is charity," or, in plainer English, "love."

The supreme purpose and object for which the whole law was given was to inculcate "love"—love for God, and love for man. Paul goes on to say that all who seek to teach or interpret the law of Moses, without understanding this main basic purpose of the whole law, "have turned aside unto vain jangling . . . understanding neither what they say, nor whereof they affirm." In other words, such interpreters have completely missed the main point of the law—which is "love." This law of love—love for God and man—is the law behind all other laws.

Paul expresses the same truth about this one supreme law of love in Romans chapter 13, verses 8, 9 and 10:

"Owe no man anything, but to love one another: for he that loveth another hath fulfilled the law.

"For this, thou shalt not commit adultery, thou shalt not kill, thou shalt not steal, thou shalt not bear false witness, thou shalt not covet; and if there be any other commandment, it is briefly comprehended in this saying, namely, thou shalt love thy neighbour as thyself.

"Love worketh no ill to his neighbour: therefore **love is the fulfilling of the law.**"

At this point someone may feel inclined to say: "You tell me that, as a Christian, I am not under the law or the commandments of Moses. Does this mean that I am free to break those commandments, and to do anything I please? Am I free to commit murder or adultery, or to steal, if I so desire?"

The answer to this is that, as a Christian, you are perfectly free to do anything that you can do with perfect love in your heart toward God and man. But, as a Christian, you are not free to do anything that cannot be done in love.

The man whose heart is filled and controlled by the love of God is free to do whatsoever his heart desires. For this reason, the apostle James twice refers to this law of love as "the law of liberty." In the Epistle of James chapter 1, verse 25, he says: "But whoso looketh into the perfect law of liberty, and continueth therein, . . . this man shall be blessed in his deed." Again, in the same Epistle, chapter 2, verse 12, he says: "So speak ye, and so do, as they that shall be judged by the law of liberty." James calls this law of love "the perfect law of liberty", because the man whose heart is filled and controlled at all times by the love of God has liberty to do exactly what he desires. Whatsoever such a man desires to do will always be in conformity with the will and nature of God, for God Himself is Love. The man who lives by this law of love is the only truly free man on the face of the whole earth—the only man who is free to do at all times what he will. Such a man needs no other law to control him.

In the same Epistle of James, chapter 2, verse 8, James gives this law of love yet another title. He calls it "the royal law". He says: "If ye fulfill the royal law according to the scripture, Thou shalt love thy neighbour as thyself, ye do well."

Why is this the "royal" law? Because the man who lives according to this law, lives indeed as a king. He is subject to no other law. He is free at all times to do whatever his heart dictates. In fulfilling this law, he fulfils all law. In all circumstances and in every relationship, toward God and man, he reigns in life as a king. Alone of all human beings, he is free from the torment of fear, for the apostle John tells us, in his first Epistle, chapter 4, verse 18: "There is no fear in love; but perfect love casteth out fear: because fear hath torment."

* * *

This analysis of what is meant by "the righteousness of the law" leads us to the following conclusion: there is no conflict or inconsistency between the standard of true righteousness put forward in the Old Testament under the law of Moses, and that put forward in the New Testament in the gospel of Jesus Christ. In each case the standard of true righteousness is one and the same; it is summed up in one word: love—love for God, and love for man. The difference between the two dispensations—the dispensation of law under Moses, and the dispensation of grace through Jesus Christ—lies not in the end to be achieved, but in the means used to achieve that end. In each case alike—both under law and under grace—the end to be achieved is love. But under the law the means used to that end is an external system of commandments and ordinances, imposed upon man from without; and under grace the means used is a miraculous and continuing operation of the Holy Spirit within the believer's heart.

The law of Moses failed to achieve its end, not because of anything wrong with the law itself, but because of the inherent weakness and sinfulness of man's fleshly nature. Paul makes this abundantly plain in the latter part of the seventh chapter of Romans. In particular, to illustrate this point, we may select Romans chapter 7, verses 12, 14, 22 and 23:

"Wherefore the law is holy, and the commandment holy, and just, and good."

"For we know that the law is spiritual: but I am carnal, sold under sin."

"For I delight in the law of God after the inward man: But I see another law in my members, warring against the law of my mind, and bringing me into captivity to the law of sin which is in my members."

The law itself is righteous and good. The man who seeks to live by the law may be perfectly sincere in acknowledging the law's standards and in seeking to live by them. But in spite of all this, the power of sin within him, and the weakness of his own fleshly nature, continually prevent him from living up to those standards.

Under the New Testament, the grace of God in Jesus Christ still directs man to the same end—love for God and love for his neighbour—but puts at man's disposal completely new and different means to attain that end. Grace begins with a miraculous operation of the Holy Spirit within the believer's heart. The result of this operation is called "being born again," or "being born of the Spirit." This experience is prophetically described in the Old Testament, in the book of the prophet Ezekiel, chapter 36, verse 26, where the Lord says to the children of Israel:

"A new heart also will I give you, and a new spirit will I put within you: and I will take away the stony heart out of your flesh, and I will give you an heart of flesh."

The effects of this inward change are further described in the book of the prophet Jeremiah, chapter 31, verses 31 and 33:

"Behold, the days come, saith the Lord, that I will make a new covenant with the house of Israel, and, with the house of Judah . . .

"But this shall be the covenant that I will make with the house of Israel; After those days, saith the Lord, I will put my law in their inward parts, and write it in their hearts; and will be their God, and they shall be my people."

This new covenant here promised by the Lord is the New Covenant of grace, through faith in Jesus Christ, which we today call the New Testament. Through this New Covenant the sinner's nature is completely changed within. The old, stony, unresponsive heart is taken away; in its place, a new heart and a new spirit are implanted within. The new nature is in harmony with God's nature and God's laws. Thus, it becomes natural for the man who has been recreated in this way by God's Spirit to walk in God's ways and to do God's will. The sovereign law of love is by the Spirit Himself engraved upon the responsive tablet of the believer's heart, and from thence it is naturally worked out in the believer's new character and conduct.

We are thus brought back to the words of Paul in Romans chapter 8, verses 3 and 4:

"For what the law could not do, in that it was weak through the flesh, God sending his own Son in the likeness of sinful flesh, and for sin, condemned sin in the flesh:
"That the righteousness of the law might be fulfilled in us, who walk not after the flesh, but after the Spirit."

The law failed to achieve God's standard of righteousness, not because of any fault in the law, but solely because of the weakness of man's fleshly nature. Under grace, the Spirit of God changes man's fleshly nature, and replaces it with a new nature, one capable of receiving and manifesting God's love.

We may sum up the basic difference between the operation of law and the operation of grace in this way: Law depends upon man's own ability, and works from without; grace depends upon the miraculous operation of the Holy Spirit, and works from within.

The great, distinctive revelation of the New Testament is that the human heart can only come under this law of divine and perfect love through the operation of God's own Holy Spirit. In Romans chapter 5, verse 5, Paul says: "And hope maketh not ashamed; because **the love of God is shed abroad in our hearts by the Holy Ghost** which is given unto us." Notice that it is not mere human love in any form or degree, but it is the love of God—God's own love—which the Spirit of God is able to shed abroad in our hearts.

This love of God shed abroad in the human heart by God's Spirit produces, in its perfection, the nine-fold "fruit of the Spirit." This "fruit of the Spirit" is the love of God manifested in every aspect of human character and conduct. It is described by Paul in Galatians chapter 5, verses 22 and 23: "But the fruit of the Spirit is love, joy, peace, longsuffering, gentleness, goodness, faith, meekness, temperance: **against such there is no law.**" Once again, Paul emphasizes that the life in which divine love is perfectly manifested in this nine-fold Spiritual fruit, does not need to be controlled by any other law. Therefore, he says: "Against such there is no law."

This law of love is thus the end of all other laws and commandments. It is the perfect law, the royal law, the law of liberty.

* * *

However, in closing this study, we must guard against leaving any impression that the love of God here spoken of is something vague, indefinite, unrealistic or sentimental. On the contrary, the love of God is always definite and practical, and according to the New Testament, love for

God and love for man alike are expressed in ways that correspond to God's own love—ways that are definite and practical.

Throughout the whole Bible, Old and New Testament alike, the supreme test of man's love for God can be expressed in one word: "obedience."

In the Old Testament, God stated this truth to His people very simply through the prophet Jeremiah. He said to them, in Jeremiah chapter 7, verse 23: "Obey my voice, and I will be your God, and ye shall be my people." True love for God is always expressed by obedience to Him.

In the New Testament likewise, Jesus, in His parting discourse to His disciples, emphasized above all other requirements this point of obedience. In John's Gospel chapter 14, He stresses this point three times in succession within the space of a few verses.

In John chapter 14, verse 15, he says: "If ye love me, keep my commandments."

Again, in verse 21 of the same chapter: "He that hath my commandments, and keepeth them, he it is that loveth me."

Then again, in verses 23 and 24 of this same chapter, He puts the two alternatives of obedience and disobedience very clearly side by side, for He says: "If a man love me, he will keep my words," and then, on the contrary: "He that loveth me not keepeth not my sayings."

In the light of these words, it is plain that for any Christian to profess love for Christ, without obeying the will of Christ revealed in His words and His commandments, is nothing but self-deception.

The supreme commandment of Christ in the New Testament is love. Without love, it is impossible to speak of obedience. But if we go on to examine the nature and the outworking of Christian love, we discover that the New Testament offers us the pattern of a life that is controlled in every aspect by this love. In order to follow this pattern, we must, with care and with prayer, study and apply every part of the New Testament's teaching.

page ninety-one

As we do this, we shall discover that the New Testament law of love has a detailed and practical application in every aspect of the believer's life. It covers the believer's own individual and personal life, his relationship both to God and to his fellow man. It directs and controls Christian marriage and the life of the Christian family, including both parents and children. It provides for the life and conduct of the Christian church; and it regulates the attitude and the relationship of the believer to secular authority and government.

As we seek to trace and to follow this pattern of divine love recorded in the New Testament, we shall prove in our experience the truth of the scripture in the First Epistle of John, chapter 2, verse 5:

"But whoso keepeth his word, in him verily is the love of God perfected: hereby know we that we are in him."

IMPORTANT RECORDED MESSAGES
BY
DEREK PRINCE
on
CASSETTES

A comprehensive series of messages by Derek Prince, carefully selected and edited, is available on tape.

They are recorded on quality cassettes.

These messages are systematically cataloged under the following headings:

- Section 1: Systematic Theology
- Section 2: Salvation & Healing
- Section 3: The Holy Spirit
- Section 4: The Christian Life
- Section 5: The Church
- Section 6: Exorcism & Deliverance
- Section 7: Prophecy

Write for FREE catalog

MESSAGES AVAILABLE ON CASSETTE

SPIRITUAL CONFLICT ALBUM I
- 1001 How Conflict Began: The Pre-Adamic Period
- 1002 The Rebellion of Lucifer
- 1003 Results Produced by Lucifer's Rebellion
- 1004 The Adamic Race: Five Unique Features
- 1005 Adam's Fall and its Results
- 1006 Results of Adam's Fall (cont'd)

SPIRITUAL CONFLICT ALBUM II
- 1007 Jesus The Last Adam
- 1008 The Exchange Made at the Cross
- 1009 Jesus Tasted Death in all its Phases
- 1010 The Cross Cancelled Satan's Claims
- 1011 Jesus the Second Man
- 1012 God's Purpose for the New Race

SPIRITUAL CONFLICT ALBUM III
- 1013 Five Ways Christ Undoes Satan's Work
- 1014 God's Program for the Close of the Age—Part I
- 1015 God's Program for the Close of the Age—Part II
- 1016 Satan's Program for the Close of the Age
- 1017 Restraining And Casting Down Satan
- 1018 Spiritual Weapons: The Blood, The Word, Our Testimony

EFFECTIVE PRAYING
- 4001 Seven Basic Conditions for Answered Prayer
- 4002 Intervening By Prayer in National Affairs
- 4003 Fasting Precipitates God's Latter Rain
- 4004 Spiritual Weapons For Spiritual Warfare
- 4005 God's Atomic Weapon: The Blood of Jesus
- 4006 Epilogue: The Glorious Church

PROPHECY
- 7001 Climax in four phases: Repentance, Refreshing, Restoration, Return of Christ
- 7002 Divine Destiny for this Nation (USA) and this generation
- 7003 Prophecy: God's Time Map
- 7004 Israel and the Church: Parallel Restoration

- Each Message is approximately one hour in length.
- A printed verse-by-verse analysis and outline is included with every tape.

OVER 115 MESSAGES ARE AVAILABLE—WRITE FOR FREE CATALOG

OTHER IMPORTANT BOOKS BY DEREK PRINCE

SELF STUDY BIBLE COURSE
A Systematic Course of Bible Doctrine in 14 lessons with
- Complete Answers
- Coordinated Memory Work
- Automatic Self Grading
- Explanatory Notes

THREE MESSAGES FOR ISRAEL
Answers to questions of vital importance for the Jewish people and for all Bible students.

THE BAPTISM IN THE HOLY SPIRIT
A scholar's exposition of the nature & purposes of this experience, seasoned with timely & practical warnings.

EXPELLING DEMONS
A brief introduction to practical demonology, explaining common symptoms of demon activity, and conditions for deliverance.

PHILOSOPHY, THE BIBLE AND THE SUPERNATURAL
A public testimony & defence of the Christian faith, given in the University of British Columbia in Canada.

APPOINTMENT IN JERUSALEM
The remarkable account of a Danish schoolteacher who had a life-changing encounter with the Holy Spirit, became the wife of Derek Prince and the mother of nine adopted daughters. In an epilogue Derek Prince makes some startling predictions about Jerusalem.

FAITH TO LIVE BY
What is faith? How can I live my life in faith? How can my faith grow stronger? Points a scriptural path to the limitless blessings of a faith-filled life.

ORDER TEACHING TAPES AND BOOKS FROM
YOUR LOCAL BOOKSTORE OR

DEREK PRINCE MINISTRIES
P. O. Box 300, Dept. B
Ft. Lauderdale, FL 33302, U.S.A.
Write for FREE catalog of Teaching
Tapes and Books by Derek Prince

B11/4-87/LRP/3m